Financial Freedom

One Rental at a Time

By

Michael Zuber

Dedication

I wrote this book for all the full-time employees who are looking and hoping for a way out of the rat race. Investing in real estate while holding a demanding full-time job is not easy, but with time and execution you can establish a better future and financial freedom.

I truly hope you enjoy this book, and that our story inspires you to embark on your own journey to improve your future.

Michael Zuber

Contents

Preface 6

Phase 1: Jump into the Game.................................8

Phase 2: Do Your Homework 31

Phase 3: The Real Estate Crash 52

Phase 4: Hit the Pause Button..............................89

21 Key Topics Every Investor Needs to Understand........101

My Journey After Retirement—One Year Later 129

Eleven Key Ideas 155

Preface

When I first started investing in real estate fifteen years ago, I searched everywhere for books written by experienced real estate investors. I looked far and wide for stories of investors with full-time jobs who actually traveled the path from first investment to financial independence, and then ultimately to retirement. I remember being fixated on the idea of retiring at a young age and enjoying life, but it was impossible to find books written from an investor's perspective, documenting their journey from full-time employment to financial independence.

In writing this book, I wanted to provide an example of someone entering the world of real estate with no special access or system, and ultimately being able to leave a full-time job. I wrote this book for all the folks who want to see that it is possible to work a full-time job, invest over time, and retire at a young age.

I chose to break up this book into two distinct sections because that is how I would have wanted to see it presented to me. I am going to begin by sharing the four distinct phases of the real estate journey I have shared with my partner, Olivia. We are going to talk about a few of our actual deals that took place during one of the most dangerous real estate cycles of the last 100 years.

Then, once I've earned at least a little bit of credibility, I am going to impart some advice on specific topics. This section will aim to answer some various questions I have received over time. It will address specific topics that I consider essential to the investor's journey, as I wanted to offer the content of our story and our advice in an easy-to-consume manner.

Our account will take you through nearly two decades of investing—2003 to 2018—and it will highlight actual investment properties and document their full story during our ownership. I will also take care to touch on beliefs I held at the start of our journey, including erroneous ones, and discuss how they evolved over time.

This book is not a get rich quick story, nor is it a sales pitch promising a magic system. I am not using this book as a platform to sell you training or anything of the sort. It is simply the story of one investor's journey over fifteen years, and serves as a real-life example that you too can use real estate investing to retire from your full-time job.

As you will see, real estate investment is a team sport, and like many team sports, there is one MVP. In my case, that's my partner Olivia. She was with me when we started investing, and is happily retired side-by-side with me now. I know very little for certain these days, but something I can say without hesitation is that I wouldn't be retired, financially independent, and writing this book if I didn't have her unwavering support each and every day.

Now what do you say we get started?

Phase 1: Jump into the Game

The first phase of our journey started with a commitment to embark on a voyage of unknown length, unknown challenges, and unknown outcome. Sounds ominous!

When Olivia and I decided to jump in, we knew next to nothing, we had no idea how long this was going to take, and we lacked any sort of real estate investing support group or connections that we could call on and ask questions. We were simply on our own and we were 100% okay with that.

The only thing we had was a desire to be financially free and we held on tight. We had no idea it would take nearly twenty years, we knew next to nothing about the real estate cycle that was in front of us, and we had no way to predict the twist and turns of the real estate investing game that would try and stop our journey.

In the end, the first part of this book is about our journey up the mountain of financial independence. We chose to write it because we wanted to leave our path marked for others to see.

When we started, we actively searched for autobiographies and stories about successful real estate investors, but we couldn't find many. The ones we did find seemingly pushed an agenda or a system in which we were not interested. Specifically, we had chosen to invest in real estate part-time while working demanding full-time jobs, and we could not find examples of folks who had done this successfully.

We hope this book helps other full-time employees understand what is possible, and establish at least a flicker of hope that they too can complete their own journey to financial independence.

Before Our Decision to Invest in Real Estate

Before jumping into real estate investing, I thought my route to retirement was paved with stock market gold. I was in my twenties and day trading stocks like an idiot. Please always remember that all boats rise in a rising market, and you can feel like a genius up until the moment you are not. I lost most of my early nest egg to stock trading (essentially gambling), and I deserved to lose every penny as an ignorant layperson who had no business investing in the stock market.

It was after a particularly rough week that I went to 100% cash and drove to a bookstore looking for investment books. I knew there had to be a better way.

Why Real Estate Investing?

I knew that I had to make a choice and bet on one vehicle to achieve financial freedom. I didn't think it was wise to focus on different types of investments, as it would be difficult to scale.

I knew I wasn't going to start a company, patent an invention, or do anything that would cause a one-time massive liquidity event, so I had to pick the slow and steady route. I also knew that I needed passive income that I could earn part-time, as I had a very demanding job with worldwide travel requirements. I found myself frequently working 80+ hours per week, and quickly realized that my only option was real estate investing.

Early on, I found the notion of allocating select pieces of time to real estate very exciting. My "Plan B" was to be an employee all my life and live the 9-to-5 dream (read: nightmare) with two-week vacations just like everyone else. I didn't like Plan B.

The Most Important Thing

The following is the most important thing you must do before you get started buying or even researching investment properties. If you have a significant other, you must, without a doubt, sit down with him or her and have a long discussion about why you want to do this, what it means for both of your futures, and how long it could take.

As you will read elsewhere in this book, it took Olivia and I nearly two decades to put our portfolio together in a place where we both could retire comfortably. I am convinced that if we were not in the same place mentally regarding our plans, we would have taken one of the many off-ramps that lead to the destruction of your dreams.

The path you are considering doesn't offer clear signs of meaningful progress for quite a while, as it takes time to secure enough properties to balance out the ups and downs of the market. It takes faith, belief, and constant affirmation that you are on the right path. If you don't have that from the start as a team, the first or second bump in the road will lead to a fight. Believe me, real estate investing is great, but it tests you all the time.

What Kind of Investor Are You?

There is one question I want to answer right off the bat: given the flood of property-flipping reality shows on TV, you may ask, "Why should I be a landlord when I can just flip my way to financial success?"

This is a fair question. The short answer is that, at best, flipping produces chunks of cash at odd intervals as opposed to monthly rent checks that show up on a consistent basis. I don't know about you, but my bills show up monthly and electric companies don't tend to wait for intermittent chunks of cash to show up on my end.

However, the biggest reason we never chose to become flippers is that *flipping is a full-time job*. I know several wildly successful flippers and I can tell you they work ridiculously hard. They seem to be constantly working on at least one project all the time while simultaneously scouting out the next opportunity. The work/life balance of your average flipper is not great, and I did not want the extra headaches or have to rely on some third party to monitor our flips. I had a very demanding full-time job, and the last thing I wanted was another one. Believe me, flipping houses is a job!

Now I must come clean: we did flip one house, and I want to share that story since I promised to tell you everything.

We decided to flip a property because of an artificial outside force that arrived in the form of an $8,000 government-issued credit for first-time buyers. As the real estate market continued to slide, the government had to do something to ease all the pain and damage occurring across America as a result of the real estate crash.

In an attempt to alleviate this instability, the federal government created a tax credit to entice first-time buyers to jump in the market.

The attempt was admirable, but as someone who was in the market every day, I knew that although demand might go up a small percentage, it could never match the huge supply of houses hitting the market every month.

We happened to be in contract for a great single-family home when this credit was announced, and like a sugar high, the market changed almost overnight. People seemed to believe that this was a sign the market had already hit rock bottom and that only appreciation and stability lay ahead.

We were skeptical, anticipating that the high would be short-lived and peter out in a matter of months. We decided to just accept the artificial gain and flip the house.

The house we had in contract almost doubled in value from the moment we put the property in escrow to the day we closed, so we invested a little extra in the make-ready cost and quickly listed the property for sale. The house went into escrow for 90% more than the original asking price, and we walked away with more capital to continue buying when the sugar high wore off.

Watch for Outside Forces—But Don't Stress Over Them

Over the course of your investment career, there will be times when outside forces make an impact on your investing journey. They could come in the form of tax code changes, a first-time buyer credit like the one above, or some other unforeseen event.

My words of advice are this: Don't stress over things you can't control.

Your journey is long enough as it is, and you don't need to carry the weight of extra stress or concerns. When an external event occurs, take a moment or two to see if it really impacts you. Most external events affect the market in general and don't really impact the individual.

However, if the external event creates an artificial pop in prices, don't be afraid to take the profit.

I often think about that house we flipped, as it was the only property we bought as a piece of our rental portfolio that we ended up selling instead. Then I remember that selling the house actually gave us the capital to buy two additional properties while the artificial high wore off and the market continued to sink lower and lower.

Our Rule of Thumb

In our first year, our rule of thumb for investing was very different than it is today; but as promised, I want to provide a full picture of our experience.

In the beginning, the only rule of thumb that real estate books seemed to endorse was the infamous 1% rule. This rule claimed that if you could buy a house for $100,000 or less and then rent it out for $1,000 or more a month, you were golden.

I don't know where this rule originated, but after twenty years of investing I can tell you that it's too simplistic and can even be dangerous if you aren't aware of other factors. However, at the time we felt like the 1% rule was some sort of secret decoder ring—to us, as novice investors, the math seemed so easy and straightforward.

Unfortunately, we can blame the 1% rule for the fact that when we first started, we found zero deals in over a year. You see, we live in Silicon Valley, where it has probably been about fifty years since there has been a property listed for under $100,000. Prices here are out-of-this-world expensive, for which the 1% rule failed to account.

We ended up spending countless weekends and evenings looking for the magic listing that would meet our 1% rule, and we never found it in Silicon Valley.

Why Fresno?

After months of searching for this mythical 1% property, Olivia and I held a meeting around the kitchen table to discuss what we should do. We could either stay true to the rule we had read about in books, or we could ignore it, as we were growing restless with our lack of investments.

(Side note: if you ever have the thought, "I need to invest in something ASAP!" please stop yourself. Investing out of impatience is usually a terrible idea.)

Okay, back to our story. It was Olivia (my MVP) who brought up the obvious flaw in our logic above. We didn't have just two options. We actually had a third option: we could decide to stay true to our 1% rule, but instead expand our search beyond our immediate area. Our initial mistake was our assumption that we had to invest in a property located within thirty minutes of our home because, shoot, that's just what you do, right?

Wrong!

We agreed that we at least wanted to be able to drive to our properties and back in a day. It could be a long day, but we had to be able to get there and back within twenty-four hours without having to get on an airplane.

I can already hear some of you saying, "You don't get it, there's nothing close to me! My local real estate market is too hot/too cold!"

Sure, maybe all of that is true, but again, remember my promise to you? I committed to telling you our story and what worked for us.

I believe that out-of-town investing can work as long as your team on the other side is professional and you have a system of checks and balances in place, but please never invest in a market you are not willing to go see. If you aren't willing to travel there, then why would you want to invest there?

With this in mind, we took out a map of California and started drawing circles: first at a sixty minute travel distance, then ninety minutes, then two hours, and then finally three hours from our home. It was this last circle that gave us Fresno as an option. We looked at other markets inside the other circles, but found that none of the other cities routinely hit our 1% Rule.

At first glance, Fresno offered several properties, and the further we dug in offered many more. We found that Fresno had a large population, a diverse employment base, and a lot of other promising attributes that made us feel like we had finally found the market that would lead us to financial freedom.

Do We Still Use the Same 1% Rule?

The short answer is no. The 1% ruled served us well in the beginning, as it allowed us to take the emotion out of investing. For example, it didn't matter if the property had great curb appeal, a new kitchen, or was painted our favorite color. If it did not meet our standards, we weren't interested.

However, over time we learned that there were other ways to compare properties, and that purchase price was only one factor to consider when making an acquisition.

Allow me to explain.

We now review our investments based on either *yield* or *return on cash invested*. By "cash invested," I mean any down payment, closing cost, and most importantly, all repair costs required to make a unit rent-ready.

Let me give you an example:

Property on "A Street"

List price: $150,000.

Down payment with standard bank financing is 20% or $30,000.

We will assume 2% in closing costs, or $3,000.

Make-ready cost is $15,000.

In this example, we have put $48,000 to work to acquire the property.

Let's say the expected year positive cash flow from rent is $2,400 (or $200 a month). Now divide that by $48,000 and you have a 5% return on cash invested.

Sure, this is not a perfect formula. Every property offers its own unique story once you own it, but understanding the yield gives us a way to compare potential opportunities.

What if the expected monthly or yearly cash flow is a *negative* number? In that case, run. You just found an "alligator" property. Never ever buy an alligator property.

An alligator property is a property that requires you to feed it with cash every month. Avoid investing in these, as they will significantly reduce your chances of long-term success. Don't try to rationalize it by telling yourself that you can afford an alligator property or two, as I promise you one thing: if you own a few, you will stop investing and you will not be successful long term. Sorry to be so harsh, but if you take only one thing away from this book, it is this:

Never, ever buy a property you have to feed every month!

Understanding the potential yield of different investment options allows us to compare all types of properties, including single-family homes, duplexes, and multi-unit apartment buildings. We hear people refer to this as "cash on cash return," but we simply think of the investment property as a *yield producer*.

Our yield rule also allows us to get creative in the way we make offers. Remember all the out-of-pocket cash from above? What if you found a way to reduce some of these costs?

Maybe you can request that the seller take back a second at closing for $15,000 at only 6% interest. What if you asked for a $6,000 credit at closing for part of the make-ready cost? In the end, there are countless ways you can control out-of-pocket cash, and therefore countless ways to increase your yield on out-of-pocket cash.

Can I Succeed Without a System?

Over the past twenty years, I have seen hundreds of infomercials, "fix-and-flip" shows, and "experts" offering systems or training in the form of upsell programs. I have read over one hundred books on real estate investing and I have attended multiple workshops and classes.

Please know that I don't believe in programs that exist only to upsell people who are hungry for some secret magical system that is always just a couple of thousand dollars away.

I admit that there are a few people who have found success with promotional flyers and mailings, but that approach has never been for me and it should not be for the readers of this book, as we already have full-time jobs.

Here is my secret.

Ready?

I've purchased all but two of my properties straight out of the Fresno MLS, which is available through local agents' public websites. I had zero special access, no mailer system, and no local wholesalers feeding me deals. I simply reviewed the MLS regularly and made offers on properties that were available to the public. This only worked because I reviewed the MLS all the time, and was willing to write offers that gave us solid yields.

Depending on the market, we might see a hit rate of anywhere from 1 in 20 to 1 in 50, as some markets are stronger for buyers and others are stronger for sellers. To complete the picture, I bought one of the two properties referenced above from an auction site during the worst of the market crash, and the other directly from a bank when they saw me investing in the property next door.

We can close with the takeaway that hard work and consistency are far more important than having access to some system with a huge time and money requirement. Instead of pouring your time into convoluted systems, just focus and learn your market.

Where Can I Find Deals?

I addressed this above, but I feel that this detail was so important to our success that I want to cover it again. We found all but two of our deals in the Fresno MLS, which is offered online, for free, by many local real estate agents. We had no special access, no pipeline of pocket listings, and no system or team bringing us opportunities.

Specifically, I want to make it clear that you can absolutely leave your full-time job without relying on any sort of special access. There are plenty of market research methods that are free and available to the public, and you can absolutely utilize these to become a very successful real estate investor.

Understand Your Goal

Unsurprisingly, I have had many friends and coworkers reach out and ask for my advice on real estate investing. They generally ask about the size of our portfolio, or how long it took us to reach financial freedom through investing. I answer all of these questions, but I also tell them that there is only one question that really matters in my mind.

I believe the most important question to ask yourself is, "What is your goal for monthly positive cash flow?" I sometimes refer to this as "understanding your monthly nut"; in other words, if you didn't have your W2 income, what would your monthly expenses be without sacrificing your standard of living? I want to talk about this because the size of your real estate portfolio isn't especially important, but your monthly goal will become the North Star on your path to retiring from your job.

Don't Splurge or Get Cocky

I am happy to report that, through the years, Olivia and I held firm and never splurged on extras during our investment journey. This means that we never took excess cash flow, refi money, or other real estate cash to buy a fancy car, upgrade our primary residence, or go on expensive vacations.

This was very hard to do, since we had plenty of opportunities to use our profits to reward ourselves, but that was not our goal. Instead, we watched friends and family buy really nice cars, upgrade their houses, and take some pretty spectacular vacations while we were quietly using that cash for down payments, make-ready costs, and other real estate items.

I remember having many talks with Olivia about potentially moving to a bigger house, or maybe "just upgrading the kitchen." We chose to pass each time, instead buying another income-producing asset in accordance with our long-term plan.

I would also like to address my use of the word "cocky" there in the section title. I've seen plenty of real estate investors get carried away with how talented and smart they thought they were when their investments were rewarded by a minor uptick in the market.

After my experience investing in stocks, I knew what was really going on; the market was simply rising, taking all ships with it. Predictably, as soon as the market turned negative, many of these investors found themselves owning alligators that ate their monthly cash and left them in really bad shape.

I strongly suggest that if you ever feel like you are the best investor in the world, you look in the mirror and get humble fast. I promise you that the market will change, and it will hurt if you're not ready.

Understanding the Lending Market

After years of investing, I have come to appreciate the importance of understanding the market of real estate investment financing. I had never appreciated this until I saw the down market become a problem for my acquisition strategy.

For the first five or so years of my real estate investing career, I found bank loans to be easy to acquire, but then I started to see things change. I went from living in a world of "sure you can have a loan, no problem!" to "no, you own too much real estate and you can't have a loan." Frankly, for many years it felt like being a real estate investor was seen as a bad thing.

Thankfully, the frost on real estate investing has started to thaw (slowly). This means values will likely rise, as demand usually increases as financing gets easier.

Why Just Fresno?

The one question I get asked the most is, "Why stay focused on the Fresno market for all these years?" I understand the curiosity and will admit to looking at other markets during our journey, but I was not willing to give up a known market for one that was unknown. Most importantly, as long as Fresno was delivering, I was not willing to invest in building another team and learning a new market.

It takes a long time and a huge commitment to really get comfortable in a market, and I never could bring myself to jump in and invest in a second or third market. I can see the allure of pursuing new markets as appreciation spikes in different areas, but the downside is the additional time and energy that I was not willing to invest, and therefore I have stayed loyal to Fresno.

Our First Property Review

For my first property review, it's only fitting that I highlight the first property we bought. Remember that one house I referenced earlier? It was on Norris Drive and we bought it for $107,000 with a plan to rent it for $1,095, or greater than our 1% rule stated.

We had done it! We were finally landlords and officially on our way to financial independence.

Or so we thought.

As I have said before, real estate investing will test you, and wouldn't you know it, this first property tested us right out of the gate. After we closed on this house, we began executing our plan of making the property rent-ready and then listing it for lease.

After two weeks it was ready, and we had at it leased at $1,095. I can't tell you how exciting it was to jump into the world of real estate investing, spend nearly a year searching for a market that worked, actually buy a property, and finally lease it for more than 1% of its original asking price. We were on cloud nine and so excited; we could see the plan working, we had confidence in our rule of thumb, and life was good.

Until… surprise! After the first month, our new tenants never paid their rent again, and we had to evict them. It seems that the couple who moved in were going through a rough patch, and while living in our unit they decided to call it quits, and the wife took off.

I understand and have empathy for someone going through a horrible life event, but as a landlord and real estate investor it meant:

• We lost three months' of rent.

• Had to pay attorney's fees to evict the remaining tenant.

• Spent nearly three times as much money turning the unit after a successful eviction because the tenant repeatedly took out his anger on my walls and destroyed the brand new carpet we installed.

Remember, you need to be on the same page as your significant other, or this one investment could have been our last. Some people may have even taken this as a sign and sold the property, deciding to secure financial freedom some other way. However, we never wavered and kept moving forward.

After this unfortunate beginning, the house on Norris Drive actually proved to be a great first real estate investment for us.

The house routinely produced a small sliver of cash flow, although never as much as our spreadsheets predicted. However, the real power was in the fact that we owned an asset in an appreciating market and a lending environment that was wide open.

Less than two years after buying the house on Norris Drive, we refinanced the property.

Remember, we had put 20% down to buy the property and its value had risen by nearly 50%, so we saw an opportunity. We had a mortgage lender approve us for an 80/10/10 loan. This meant the lender would put an 80% first on the property followed by a 10% second, leaving us with 10% equity.

This meant two things for us.

1. We would walk away with a huge pile of cash.

2. The property would never again be a source of positive cash flow for us. Sure, I could finesse my spreadsheet to show a small positive cash flow, but in reality we had created an alligator that we had to feed every month.

Big mistake!

On the positive side, we had a lot of cash and this was our moment of truth. We could buy a nice new car, upgrade our kitchen, take a once in a lifetime trip—or we could invest in more real estate and take another step in our journey. We chose the latter, and we will discuss that in future chapters.

However, our time with Norris Drive was not yet over.

While we saw the refinance of Norris Drive as monthly cash flow that would never be positive again, a funny thing happened. Over the course of the next two years, the market went up another 50%. At this point, we couldn't find any more single-family homes that met our 1% rule, and we had huge equity in an asset that actually hurt us every month.

We were stuck!

We owned a half-dozen properties at this time and we couldn't find any more that made financial sense, so we faced a dilemma. We could buy more alligators when we already had one, and it was no fun to feed every month. We could just sit on our hands and wait, we could explore different markets, or we could just keep buying, since lenders were throwing money at us. Our loan options included negative amortization loans, which, on paper, gave us huge monthly cash flow while adding debt to the house. We considered this option but it never felt right, as I couldn't foresee achieving financial independence by growing our debt.

I just knew there was a nasty surprise lurking in those loans, and boy did I underestimate the negative impact they would have on the entire real estate market and the American economy in general, as you will see in later sections.

While we were stuck and really stressing about what to do next, another real estate investor asked us if we ever considered investing in small apartment buildings. Naively, I replied, "Sure we have! We actually own a duplex already."

I remember him politely shaking his head and saying, "No, I mean a commercial property or building with five or more units."

Perplexed, I responded, "No, why do you ask?"

He launched into a long speech about how successful real estate investing does not just mean investing in single-family homes and duplexes. He indicated that you need to look up and make sure you are investing for maximum return, and maybe, *just maybe,* given current conditions the best return did not lie in the single-family home market.

His last point was just made in passing, but looking back, it proved to be the real asset of this conversation. Why? Because banks finance one- to four-unit properties based on the buyer's eligibility, while they finance five units and above based on the given building's ability to repay.

This last statement proved to be the key. We had started looking around at small buildings and we were finding some that met our 1% rule. I remember thinking that we had done it and our journey was about to continue, if not accelerate into another gear.

This is where Norris Drive leaves us, and we learned about another important concept called the 1031 Exchange. The 1031 Exchange is an exchange of "like kind" investments comprised of many very detailed rules that must be followed, which I won't delve into here as I just want to keep this story about Norris Drive. In short, the exchange allowed us to take equity from Norris Drive and place that equity into a bigger, like-kind real estate investment without paying capital gains taxes.

We listed Norris Drive for 150% more than its original purchase price. It went into escrow the week we listed it, and after 90 days or so, we closed on a five-unit building.

Think about that. We now had five units producing 2.5 times the rent, providing real cash flow, and it cost less than some single-family homes that still rented for only $1,095 after five years. I remember thinking about this for days and going, "I don't get it, something has to be wrong! Who would invest in a house that costs more and rents for half as much?" It turns out that plenty people did, and that party ended abruptly and badly for many people.

Norris Drive was a great property for us because it offered so many lessons:

It was the start of our journey to financial independence.

It quickly tested our commitment and plan.

It showed us the dangers of owning an alligator property.

It introduced us to small multi-family homes.

It introduced us to the benefits of 1031 Exchanges.

To bookend the tale of Norris Drive, I actually had a chance to buy the same property a few years after selling it, as the new owner lost it to foreclosure and the bank was ready to deal. I made an offer but was outbid by another real estate investor.

So goes the full story of our first real estate investment property.

Phase 2: Do Your Homework

Over the years, I have had the privilege of coaching many new investors. It's always a lot of fun, and I've quickly realized that after the first couple hours, I can to start to see who is and who's not going to be successful achieving their stated goal.

I've found that if I ask the aspiring investor to repeat even half of what I've told them about our first year investing, I can tell very early on who really wants this, and who's just hopping around from investment idea to investment idea.

I asked the first couple of investors to research 100 properties, which seems like a lot until you realize that I looked at over 250 properties before I invested a single dollar. After receiving some feedback, I realized that 100 was too many, so I lowered the homework requirement to fifty.

Now, keep in mind the homework was really quite simple. I wanted to see a spreadsheet with a list of 50 properties, with the criteria the investor thought was important, and finally, a ranking of the best to worst deals. This exercise allowed us to have critical discussions, and most importantly, gave the investor a huge base of knowledge.

How about you?

Will you create a list of 50 properties, document criteria, and then rank the deals from best to worst? Note that you don't have to physically see all of them, but walking through a few never hurts. Again, I want to help you, so please do heed my suggestion and do your homework.

Key Thoughts Post-Homework

In assigning this homework, I was purposefully vague in order to see how the mind of the potential investors worked. I saw some beautiful spreadsheets, with dozens of columns and tons of facts. After letting the investors share their homework, I had to burst their bubble a little because, if you wanted to follow the same path I took, most of the items in the column just didn't matter.

When they were done, I took over with a little bit of tough love and said something like the following:

• List price means nothing; what would *you* offer?

• What are the make ready-costs of each unique property?

• What is the rent? Are you familiar with the rental market for that type of property?

• What is your yield on cash invested?

• Can you do anything to the property or adjust your offer to increase your yield?

In my world, a property's aesthetic aspects like square feet, crown molding, backyards, new kitchens, and house color don't matter. I consider the number of bedrooms, bathrooms, parking, and anything else that allows me to raise rents.

In the world of renting, where people eventually move out, all the extras on rental properties that some folks love are just added expenses.

The most important thing I hope investors take away from my homework assignment is *confidence.* I want to establish a strong foundation for future investors so they can look at properties and know exactly where a given property ranks out of all the others they have seen. I find that investors need confidence from the get-go, or they won't make a move.

Over the years I have seen three basic categories of investors.

The first type comprises the gamblers who claim to be real estate investors. They drive to a market, see five properties, make four offers, and buy three properties in a weekend without a second thought.

This might work out, but how would you know? I suppose taking action is better than being frozen in place, but not by much in my book. Instead, keep your cash sitting tight, do 30 to 60 days of basic research, and when you can look at a property and rank the deal in the top 10% or so, *then* maybe make an offer.

I remember one investor with whom I spoke had about $500,000 to invest, and within 45 days he had ten houses and nothing left. I don't know why anyone would be in that much of a hurry to buy, but it happens to part-time investors all the time. They feel they have so few chunks of time to devote to investing that they *must* buy something before they have to get back to their busy lives.

The second type of investor I often see is frozen in place. They talk a good game and even do the work, but they seem to always feel they are missing this or that bit of information. Maybe they need one more weekend of research and they will be ready. Pretty soon, this indecision becomes dissatisfaction with not finding a property, and boom, they're off to the next thing.

Finally, the last set of investors consists of the ones who really listen, ask questions, and do the work. Most of the time this group does much more work than the minimum, as they are committed to taking the journey and willing to do more than what is asked of them.

In my experience, only 10% of the people I speak with fall into this camp.

I suppose that is to be expected. Staying on task for twenty years is hard, especially during the first five to ten years. In the beginning, it can be difficult to visualize the small trickles of income turning into a river of financial independence, and it takes real belief and commitment.

It is not easy, but this book is intended to show you it is possible if you are willing to sacrifice and work hard.

Always Stay Engaged

So what do you do if you don't yet have enough money for a down payment on your first or second property? Do you get a second job? Do you work overtime? Do you drive to your first property and celebrate your success?

To all of these the answer is "No." Instead, stay engaged, and keep researching and learning your market. Keep watching your real estate market, MLS, and listings. There is a certain heartbeat to each market, and only by staying active in that market can you pick up on subtle changes.

For instance, if you only look at listings every ninety days, you won't see that certain types of houses may be coming on and off the market very fast. Remember, I had no special access; I had no real estate agent feeding me expired listings or weekly price changes. It was only by looking every day and taking notes that I could see that, for whatever reason, three bedrooms were selling faster than four bedrooms, and price points below $200,000 were hot but those above $200,000 were not.

Do not wait until you have money for a down payment to start researching and learning. In fact, when you *don't* have money to buy is the perfect time to spend extra cycles learning the market.

Be sure to stay engaged regardless of your cash position; you never know when you might pick up that extra piece of information that helps you later in your career.

People Business

For the first several years, I didn't understand just how much real estate is a people business. A successful real estate investor must have relationships with all kinds of tradespeople, real estate agents, appraisers, property managers, and attorneys. Of course, sellers, buyers, and renters will also be part of your financial voyage.

At the beginning of this book I promised to highlight my mistakes, and this is a mistake I made early on. When I started investing in Fresno real estate, the market was hot and it only got hotter for the next four to five years. I remember reading an article at one point claiming that the number of Fresno real estate agents was the highest on record.

As we will see in later sections, this type of environment is not sustainable, but it also caused me to ignore some important parts of the people business. For example, I never sent thank you notes or holiday gifts to my team or the other people who helped me the first five years. I feel terrible admitting that to you but it is true.

Now I routinely send thank-you notes to people who have helped me add properties to my portfolio, and I always send Christmas gifts to team members who help us. It feels great sending these small gifts and personal notes of thanks, and believe me, people remember these things, as so few people do them.

The Journey Is Slow

I can still remember sitting back after ten years of investing and going, "Where is this wave of amazing cash flow and when will it finally show up?" The fact was, we *were* seeing increasing cash flow, but we were also buying new properties, and any positive gains went to make-ready costs on our next unit.

I now believe that most real estate investment properties have a one-year seasoning period, and of course, this is where surprises happen.

I can't tell you how many times we had a water heater or roof leak in a new acquisition. Before you ask, we did conduct inspections during the escrow period, but these leaks happened so regularly that I now just expect the first year of any new property to have at least one, if not two unpleasant surprises.

If you're acquiring a new property every six months like we did for ten years, it might feel like no cash flow is showing up, but I promise you that it is. That wave of cash is helping you fund make-ready costs on the next acquisition.

Properties Two to Six

After buying Norris Drive, we went on to buy five additional investment properties over the next two years. Each of these properties was your standard three or four bedroom, two bath, two car garage house that rented for between $1,100 to $1,250—with one exception.

A property on Farris Drive turned into our first multi-unit property. This property was on an oversized lot and actually offered two single-family homes. Each home had its own address and water meter, and was 100% up to code.

This find was interesting for several reasons. First, its asking price put it in the top 20% of most expensive listings for the area. Second, it had a horrible photo and an even worse description on the MLS, and it had been on the market for a long time for obvious reasons. After seeing it listed for at least three months, I had to go see the property. I believed the agent and seller must have believed there was some value to the property, as no one would list that ugly photo at that asking price if there weren't something there.

My curiosity paid off when we went to go see the property, and I remember thinking I had found a diamond in the rough. Its curb appeal was just as bad as it was in the pictures, but what the photos failed to show was the value of the second house. They were also unable to show how a few thousand dollars in yard work would really make the property pop. It would literally turn an eyesore into one of the nicest houses on the block.

Remember when I talked about staying engaged in the market? This is an example of that engagement paying off. The listing was so old that when I called the agent to ask questions, he told me that the last phone call he received about the property had ben sixty days ago, and he was going to let the listing expire since it was too much work keeping the out-of-town seller up to date. I started to see more dollar signs, but he was very talkative and I kept asking questions. I learned the property was owned free and clear. It had been passed from its original owner to a child who hadn't been in Fresno for twenty years and had no interest in the property, but wanted the cash.

So I asked the agent a magic question. I asked if he would be interested in representing me, and thus double-dipping on the commission. He said of course, but he would need to verify with the seller that they were also comfortable with the arrangement. He was confident that as long as he brought a legitimate offer, it wouldn't be a problem.

I then told him I wanted to offer $30,000 less than asking, and I wanted him to take back a second mortgage of 10% of the offer price, since I needed extra cash to repair the units and make them presentable. The agent didn't think the seller would come down that low and he had no idea how they felt about carrying a note. We decided to write it up and see what happens.

Forty-eight hours later, the agent got back to me with a counter on two things that were slightly different than my offer. First, the seller was willing to come down $25,000 but not $30,000. I was excited beyond belief, as the property would have provided a cash flow at the asking price. Second, the seller wanted a five-year term rather than the ten years I asked for.

Thirty days later, we owned another great property and the largest single cash flow producer of our first six investments.

By staying engaged and asking questions, you can create what feels like once-in-a-lifetime deals. The Farris property taught me that asking price is just a number, and that you can actually get sellers to help you reduce out-of-pocket costs.

Who would have thought it possible to buy two single-family homes at nearly the same price as one! It was a great deal all around, and one I hoped to replicate many times going forward. Unfortunately, to date I have not come across the same collection of events that lead to this amazing buy, but I won't stop looking!

Odd Places to Find Capital

As I became increasingly more comfortable making acquisitions, I was very frequently left in need of more capital to make the next deal. We were saving every penny we could, but it takes a while to save up for a down payment, even if it is only 10% of the purchase price.

Over the years I have found a few unique places to raise capital, and I am sure there are many more.

The first place I looked was my 401K. Now, I am *not* giving you tax or investment advice. As promised at the start of this book, I am only recounting my own story of how I achieved financial freedom. Part of that entailed taking a loan against my 401K a couple times over a ten-year period. I don't remember the exact terms, but the process was easy. I selected my preferred repayment period, and the payments came out of my weekly check. I always opted for one-year repayment periods, as I wanted to reuse this option at least once a year if I needed to. Do note that if you leave your job before paying off a loan, you must repay it or face tax consequences. Please do your own research and talk to your tax or finance team before blindly following my example.

At some point I also considered getting a loan against my car. I owned a car that was worth around $20,000, and I knew I would be able to get a bank loan for $10,000. I never ended up going through with this, but I was ready to if the deal made sense.

Investing in an Accelerating Market

I used to hold the false belief that real estate property value only went up, but as we will see in later sections, that is just wrong. Looking back now, it's obvious that I was investing at the beginning of an accelerating up-cycle, and it was awesome. Every two years or so, all my investment properties increased by $50,000 or more. Boy, do you feel like a genius when this happens!

Let me hit the pause button on this story for a minute and share a scary fact with you. While prices went nuts for several years, asking rents never moved. Yes, a house I bought for just over the 1% rule ended up being less than .5% or even less than .33% in some cases. If you ever run into a market where prices are going up but rents are flat for years, I suggest you be very careful.

Okay, back to our story of exciting asset appreciation. It was a crazy time to invest. Properties were flying off the shelf so to speak, and most of the time for up to 10% over list price. To say it was hard to find deals in the single-family market is an understatement.

We had a choice at this point. Our first option was to repeat the first step we took with the Norris Drive property I told you about earlier. Hopefully you remember just how stupid that was.

Remember, by taking a refi, we created an alligator out of a cash flow property. We learned our lesson and we didn't want five or six alligators on our hands, so a cash-out refi was off the table. That left us with the option of looking at small apartment buildings that required commercial financing. Specifically, we decided to look for properties between five and ten units.

Surprisingly, we found a part of the market with almost no activity. For whatever reason, purchasing five units would require a different type of loan, and therefore negative amortization loans, 3% down loans, and other risky loan programs were not available.

This meant the small guys in the single-family market would ignore 5- to 10-unit properties, as they didn't fit with the financing on which these investors depended. Additionally, the big guys wanted scale and wouldn't look at any properties with under 30 units. The 5- to 10-unit market was ripe for deal-making.

Getting Into 5- to 10-Unit Apartment Properties

We found this part of the real estate market to be very calm and reassuring. Over the next 12 to 18 months, we sold every single-family home and duplex we owned and performed 1031 Exchanges to small apartment buildings. Take a look how the math worked out pre- and post-exchange:

Property #	Rent	Cash Flow	# of Units	Rent	Cash Flow
House 1	$1,095	-$150	5 Units	$2,700	$500-$650
House 2/3	$1,000	$150	7 Units	$3,600	$600-$750
House 4/5	$2,200	$200	10 Units	$7,000	$1,200-$1,500
Duplex 1	$1,900	$400	10 Units	$6,000	$1,500-$1,800

As you can see, we used the 1031 exchange to significantly increase our unit count, our total rent, and most importantly, our cash flow. We went from seeing a trickle of less than $1,000 to seeing over $3,500 in a good month.

I had no idea what a 1031 Exchange was when I first entered the world of real estate, but through research and sheer determination to keep buying, we found a way to significantly increase our asset base without spending one more dollar out of pocket.

Looking back on this, I wish I could tell you I knew what was just around the corner, but that would be untrue. Instead, I will just say that we couldn't make the numbers work in the single-family market by any stretch of the imagination, and we therefore sold everything to move every dollar into small apartment buildings.

Note that once again, we had a choice. We could have taken five more cash-out refinances and pulled about $300,000 out of our portfolio to buy five more single family homes, or we could have just spent the money.

We know a lot of people that did this. They felt like they knew the single-family market, and who doesn't like seeing their net worth increase every month? If we would have done this, I promise you we would have lost all ten properties. They were not cash flow positive, and any loan type that made them cash flow positive for two to three years would have been a joke that led to foreclosure.

We could have sat on our hands and been happy with what we had. We didn't have to play in this game we could have sat out, kept our six properties, and waited for better times. We didn't like this option, as we were not making enough money to support ourselves, and stopping so soon felt like failure.

Instead, we decided that the single-family market was nuts at the moment, and chose to look at a different segment of rental units. We then sold all our properties at or near their peak, and moved the equity to these apartment buildings. This worked beautifully, as we got to keep all that artificial equity from ridiculous housing prices in the apartment buildings while prices started to fall off a cliff in the single-family home market.

In the end, there is more than one real estate market, and if one doesn't make sense, go look at another one. This saved us, and more importantly, jump-started our real cash flow growth.

How Artificial Rules Saved Us

As I shared above, the small apartment rental market saved us. We could have lost everything if we had stayed in the single-family market any longer. I don't know why you can buy a 4-unit property with residential mortgages but you have to buy a 5-unit building with commercial mortgages, and I don't care. All I know is this seemingly artificial rule rescued my real estate investing career and I would not be financially free without it.

From my perspective, commercial mortgages and financing just mean a lot more paperwork and require more down payment and true "skin in the game." As we were selling our single-family homes, an investor could get a 3% down neg-am loan with a 2% starter interest rate. However, a commercial loan required 30% or 35% down, as the lenders had a whole different set of rules and guidelines aimed at protecting the lender.

I am left smiling when I look back on this part of our investing timeline, because I now know that a little more paperwork and a real down payment meant we were being active in a market with very little competition. We got great prices and had ultimate security while the lenders made sure the building would yield a cash flow given the large down payment.

I have referred to this switch in the past as "just a lucky break," but it wasn't. We couldn't make the numbers work, we didn't want another alligator property, and we knew we weren't even close to leaving the real estate world, so we kept looking and we found 1031 Exchanges and small apartment buildings at the perfect time.

Signs of an Overheating Market

Sometimes not making an offer is the right answer.

Allow me to list a few sample headlines that should indicate that you may want to pause and check to see if you are in for trouble:

Record number of new real estate agents.

Most new loans get funded with less than 5% down.

Dinner and work conversations always turn to the latest flip.

People with no real estate background quit their day jobs to become real estate flippers.

Cash out refinances hit record highs.

Buyers outnumber sellers five to one.

The Pause Button

I don't like to admit it, but sometimes hitting the pause button on new acquisitions is the right idea. After we sold all of our initial units and 1031 Exchanged our way into small apartment buildings, we were stuck. The single-family market was still ridiculously high (and about to collapse), and buying our next small apartment building would require a much larger down payment that could take up to a year to save.

As per usual, we had some choices. We could roll the dice, buy just one more house and see what happened, or sit tight and save for a down payment on our next apartment building. If we had chosen the former we would have lost that house for sure, as the market was right at its peak as we were considering this.

I like to call this one year a "pause button" for us. Over the course of our careers, we made real estate investments during twelve out of our fifteen years of investing, with this being the first year we did nothing other than our 1031 Exchanges. We just watched the market and saved all the money we could until the single-family market blew up and prices quickly collapsed.

Unlike our switch to commercial apartment buildings, I will refer to this as a "lucky break," as I had no idea what was about to happen. All I knew was that I needed to save up for a big down payment on my next small apartment building. What I didn't see coming was the collapse of the single-family market, which left me in shock like everyone else. The speed of the collapse and the damage it caused was frightening to watch.

On the upside, it was incredibly lucky that we had already moved our investments from single-family homes to small apartment buildings. Sure, the buildings were worth less on paper, but I didn't care; I was actually able to raise rents by nearly $100 per unit, as more people wanted small apartments to live in after losing their homes or being discouraged by the rough economy from buying houses.

Property Review—Farris Drive

For this property review, I want to talk about the building on Farris Drive that I mentioned earlier in this chapter. I have already discussed how I secured what ended up being the best deal of the first six we made. However, I did not finish the story.

We owned this property for about three years, and we sold it for more than double what we paid for it. During our ownership, the property was a dream. We performed the initial yard clean up and tree trimming, and then rented out both units almost immediately. Over the course of three years, the same initial tenants lived in both units and we had very few repair costs. I think one water heater broke at some point, but that was about it.

We learned that good single-family homes in nice areas don't turn over very often, and thus are solid additions to any portfolio.

When the market was near its peak, we sold Farris Drive and 1031 Exchanged the equity into a 10-unit building we still own to this day. The equity from Farris meant we did not need to pull any cash out of our pocket to buy the 10-unit building, and we have been receiving positive monthly cash flow every month.

Like Norris Drive in my first property review, I made an offer on Farris Drive after it went to foreclosure, but was beat out by another investor.

In the end, Farris Drive taught us a lot. It taught us to watch listings for clues about what could be a deal in the making. It taught us about the beauty of quality houses in nice neighborhoods, and we learned to move the equity to another asset when the market got too hot.

Challenges for Early Stage Real Estate Investors

I thought I would close our second chapter with a discussion on early challenges that can throw you for a loop and knock you off your path if you're not careful.

Spreadsheet Cash Flow

The most obvious early mistake is finessing your personal spreadsheet until it indicates a cash flow. I promise you this much: if you don't see a fat cash flow without any fudging of the numbers, then you are adding an alligator to your portfolio. Don't do that. Alligator properties are no fun, as I learned after getting a cash-out refi on my first investment property. Keep yourself honest when creating your spreadsheets, and avoid this mistake.

Lack of Reserves

Some investors talk a good game about having reserves, and then when they happen to find the "deal of the century," they suddenly raid their reserves. If this happens, these are not true reserves but instead a secondary pile of investment money. Instead, be sure to have an actual reserve and *never use it to buy a property*. Reserves exist to protect you and your entire portfolio should you encounter any surprises, and believe me, you will.

Lack of Consistent Communication

As I shared earlier, you will need to communicate with your significant other about your investment plans and make mutual decisions. My hope is that you heard me and made sure to reach 100% agreement on your goals before you started. Believe me when I say that communication can't end there. It needs to be consistent, and you should both be involved in the process. You are embarking on a journey that can take twenty years to complete, so you had better get used to talking about your portfolio and the real estate market. It is going to be part of your lives for a long time.

Feeling Too Much

I have had over 1,000 tenants since becoming a landlord, and all I can say is I have heard every excuse possible for missed rent. It is hard and I feel for everyone, but at the end of the day I need to make my mortgage payment and they need to pay their rent. If they can't, they can leave or face eviction, as we must secure rent for our units or we lose the property back to the bank. I no longer listen to the excuses, and instead just execute the same three-day late policy and begin the eviction process as documented in the lease.

Phase 3: The Real Estate Crash

This next challenge we encountered could have either ended our journey or accelerated us on our path away from relying on a full time job.

Before diving in, I feel compelled to acknowledge that the real estate crash was horrible. It left many people in a bad place and caused a lot of pain that I hope never to see again.

However, as you will see, the real estate crash gets a lot of credit for enabling us to exit the workforce early. Hold on tight as we review the crash from our perspective.

Real Estate Doesn't Go Up Forever

Remember back in Phase Two, when we had to hit the pause button for the first time and refrain from buying a single investment property for nearly a year because we had to start saving for significant down payments if we wanted to buy additional small apartment units?

As we executed our plan to save for our next large down payment, we stayed engaged in our market as advised in Phase One of our story. This allowed us to keep tabs on just how crazy the market was getting. We could not believe the things we were hearing. Below are just a sample of a few that still scare us to this day:

"I can support eight investment properties that have a negative cash flow of $200 a month each, and I will retire in ten years."

I seriously had an investor tell me this. Their plan was to buy eight properties that had negative cash flow baked into their financial model. I remember the investor being very proud of the fact that he could support eight negative cash flow properties (in other words, eight alligators). I didn't know what to say at the time, as I had created a single alligator property back in the day and it was incredibly painful every month. I couldn't imagine why anyone would willingly feed eight hungry alligators. As you might suspect, the investor lost all these properties. Who wants to feed alligators every month when they are worth half of what you owe, and you see no possible way to get out from under this crushing debt?

"I quit my six-figure job to flip houses in a market three states away."

There is so much wrong with this one quote! Where do I begin? It appears that the investor thinks the rules of understanding a local real estate market don't apply to them. Technology is great and the ability to do real research online is powerful, but come on. If you are going to leverage your hard-earned money, go spend some time getting firsthand experience in the market. If you are not comfortable in that market, don't invest there. I promise it will try to scare you out quickly after taking a large percentage of your nest egg.

This investor quit their job before even getting one property under their belt! Can you believe that? This is so wrong on so many levels that it's hard for me to understand why anyone would think this is a good idea. Question for you: do you know what criteria banks look at when they are looking to fund a residential real estate loan?

It's simple. They are evaluating the likelihood of getting paid back, and the number one factor in being able to pay back a loan is the borrower having a job or W2 income.

Banks love lending to W2 employees who make six figures.

Do you know to whom they *don't* like to lend money?

You guessed it! Banks aren't huge fans of lending to unemployed dreamers full of hope and boundless energy, who have no experience and no documented success. In this case, the investor spent about ninety days trying to make their plan work, just stumbling around before going back to another W2 job.

On the plus side, they got lucky—they never invested a dime in real estate and only lost time. The unfortunate part is that when they went back to work, their experience had soured them on real estate investment and they gave up the opportunity to profit from the real estate crash.

"Sure, I have negative cash flow now, but in two years the prices will double and I will sell."

I probably heard a hundred variations of this quote in a twelve-month period. This is odd logic. We had been in the real estate market for probably five or six years at this point, and we had seen all of our properties at least double. While we did have real experience in prices doubling as I described in earlier sections, the rents never budged and we ended up selling (read: 1031 Exchanging) everything because the simple math did not work out.

Every time we heard someone say this we would think, "One of us is going to be right and the other is going to be spectacularly wrong." We didn't know which, and we knew all too well that we could be wrong; who was to say prices wouldn't double, or even triple again?

Well, as the section heading says, real estate prices couldn't go up forever.

"I have to buy five houses this weekend."

I remember hearing this quote and having only one question: "Why?" For whatever reason, this investor was so convinced and so committed to real estate investing that they wanted to take all their liquid cash and put it to work immediately.

The problem is, real estate is not like stocks or other investments. There are two big reasons you wouldn't normally commit all of your capital in one weekend.

First, you have not done your homework and therefore have no idea how to distinguish a good deal from a bad deal.

Second, real estate investing is not very liquid, should you need your capital back. There are tons of transaction costs when you sell, and the real estate market cycle can be nasty and unforgiving if you have to sell at the wrong time.

Please don't treat real estate investing like stocks and properties like day trades, as this mindset only guarantees losses.

"I plan to retire on real estate investments in two years."

I will admit to being a little upset when I heard this one. We had already been investing for six years or so, and I knew we were not even close to being financially free. I was like, "Good for you. Did you know that we have been in the game for six years and we just completed some great 1031 Exchanges that increased our cash flow, and we are still not even close to being done?"

I never fully understood why they thought two years was their magic number, but I was excited for them and their belief in real estate investing as their path to success. Unfortunately, their investment high wore off quickly when they had no luck making the numbers work after a mere ninety days of effort, and they turned their attention to something else without ever buying an investment property.

My personal favorite:

"The real estate market never goes down! Why not put every penny to work regardless of price? Time will make everything a good investment."

This quote, and many like it, were thorns in my side for a long time during our self-induced "acquisition pause," as I wasn't sure if they were right and I was wrong. It really bothered me that so many people were just jumping in and making a killing on paper when I was stuck on the sidelines saving money for our next small apartment building. This one idea ate at me for months, and then it happened: the first cracks in the real estate market started to show, and I felt vindicated.

Real estate doesn't go up forever, especially when there are outside forces in the financial market packaging and selling junk loans with no chance of payback on the open market.

As you may recall, the industry actually offered loans that they openly called "liar loans." Yes, it turns out that some mortgage brokers encouraged applicants to lie on their applications. No one was checking the facts on the forms, so why not? Fill it out, fib on the numbers, and collect a bonus for processing another loan. The banks didn't really care, and they sold the loans to Wall Street brokers, who packaged them into bundles and sold them.

I never fully understood the details of all the slicing and dicing that went on, but at the street level where I was operating, I could just feel something was off; the numbers did not support prices, and I could never get myself comfortable settling with a bad deal or buying an alligator.

In Real Estate, Negative Momentum Is Dangerous

Momentum can be a powerful thing. Negative momentum can lead to several outcomes that feed on themselves and produce even more negativity.

During our self-induced pause on buying, I remember seeing the first cracks in the market. Reported delinquencies rose, and the early "liar loans" started to reset after their introductory two-year period.

Once the momentum started building, the negative market trend became a race to the bottom, leaving hundreds of thousands of people in terrible shape. This negative momentum fed on itself for years.

As most trends do, it started slowly, and the signs were only obvious if you were paying attention to the market at all times (as recommended in Phase One). Suddenly, listings started to read, "Seller Motivated" and "Make an Offer, any Offer!" Active listings doubled and then tripled as sellers were rushing to the door and buyers disappeared.

This trend only got worse, as 90-day delinquencies became REOs. These were the properties the banks had to repossess from sellers who did not pay as agreed on their mortgage. The banks would then sell the properties themselves.

Once the first REOs started appearing in the Multiple Listing Service, the negative momentum really started to pick up. Let's look at an example of a listing I followed for several months. The listing, an attractive home in a nice area, started at $225,000, and would rent for $1,100 to $1,200.

About six weeks after I saw the listing for the first time, the description and price changed.

It now read "Seller desperate, must sell," and the price dropped to $199,000. Price drops continued for another 90 days until the listing finally disappeared. I think the last price I saw was $149,000. I remember thinking that was a little expensive, but I could see how that might have been an acceptable first investment for someone.

About 90 days later, I saw that same house listed as an REO for $99,000. It turned out the property had gone through foreclosure and the bank was now selling it. Again, I feel compelled to remind you that I had no special access, no foreclosure list, and no real estate agent feeding me weekly statistics. I simply had my daily review of online listings, my notes on properties, and any information available on the internet.

When I saw this property listed again for $99,000, I was shocked; that was more than half off the original asking price I had seen seven months earlier. I didn't know what to make of it, but I knew that had to hurt someone. Little did I know just how much pain was represented by that single example, as the scenario repeated at an ever-increasing scale and frequency for years.

Due to our pause in acquisitions, Olivia and I had saved a nice chunk of down payment money by this point. I remember thinking that I had better pay attention, as I had never seen this type of price drop before. It was alarming to see a quality house start at $225,000 and drop to $99,000 in less than a year. This was new to me, but over time it would become the norm with the market offering up even more extreme examples.

When Everyone Gets Negative, It's Time to Get Greedy

Perhaps the most drastic change we witnessed was in the general attitude towards real estate. It felt like in one weekend, everyone went from talking about their latest purchase or flip to no one wanting to even mention real estate. People love to talk about their winnings, but no one likes to talk about the pain they are suffering.

People were giving up on real estate left and right, which caused a ripple effect and the cycle of negativity to continue. I have never before witnessed a change in attitude so quickly and so drastically. I remember sitting back and asking, "Should I sell? Did something change? Where does all this negativity go?"

After taking inventory of our thoughts and experiences, we came to two conclusions.

First, we would not sell anything. The value of our apartments had fallen a little, which meant our net worth took a hit, but our cash flow increased as rents went up. We cared a lot more about cash flow than some number on paper indicating net worth.

The second thing we agreed on was to extend our investment hiatus until we had more information about what was actually going on in the market. We liked the prices being offered, as they were actually in many cases below the cost of our first investment on Norris Drive. However, the negativity and the speed of market decline scared us too much to take action until we had more data.

We continued to save money during this period, and we started to do some research on past real estate declines. We read about the crash in the 1980s, then local crashes like the oil bust in Texas and the So Cal crash caused by the military pulling out of the area.

During the course of our research, we found a couple things to be true across the board.

Once real estate values start their decline, prices continue falling to ridiculous levels.

In every market crash story we read about, we saw example after example of houses being sold for less than 50% of their one-time value. Additionally, they all showed that being early on the price declines was just silly, as price drops of this size do not come and go within a six-month window.

Eventually prices dropped to unbelievably low levels, and big money players would come in and buy everything. When this happens you're out of luck, as these investors will buy everything, even sight unseen. They're playing the numbers game and are willing to buy a couple of dogs in order to stock their portfolios full of diamonds.

While the $99,000 price I highlighted above felt like a steal, it became obvious from our research that it was just a harbinger of the pain to follow. As supply increases and demand disappears, there is only one thing a seller can do: lower prices. Banks with ever-growing portfolios of REOs started reducing prices every 30 days like clockwork, which led to even more price drops.

This realization meant we could keep saving while staying active in the market via research and daily reviews of the MLS. We knew that at some point we would need to take our fingers off the pause button and jump back into the market, but it just wasn't time yet.

The Bottom

In each market decline example we saw, prices eventually stabilized before starting to increase at a decent rate. Unfortunately, it was impossible to predict how far away from the bottom you were at any given moment.

This meant that we would have to stick our toes back in the water and start buying again at some point, but not yet. It was clear from our research that no bottom had ever been reached within a year of the downturn. Most of our research showed that it took years to form, but when it did, the bounce was sudden and quick. We knew that once we decided to jump in, we had to be aggressive and keep buying, with faith that a bottom would eventually form.

We also needed to come to terms with the fact that there would be no alarm bell screaming, "Bottom in! Start buying!" On the contrary, we expected a large outside force to come in and change the market seemingly overnight.

Investors Have Eight-Year Memories

The last thing we identified in our research was that after reaching its bottom, every market recovered and went on to new highs. I am not sure where I heard the quote above, but it is pretty accurate in my experience. Individual investors seem to have eight-year memories, while the real estate market lives in cycles of ten to twelve years.

This means it takes individuals about eight years to forget the bloodbath they experienced in the last down-cycle, compelling them to jump on the next up-cycle as it reaches its end.

Think about that for a moment. You ride a market down-cycle all the way to the bottom, a floor is put in, and you don't jump back in until the up-cycle is half over, meaning you're getting half the deal you could have when the market was at the bottom.

Should I Sit Back and Wait?

Waiting with the knowledge there will be no clear sign that it's safe to get back in the water can be anxiety-inducing. As we were saving increasing amounts of money, we were convinced we would get back into single-family homes, since the market was much better than we had ever seen. However, we knew we didn't have unlimited capital and we wanted to be cautious without standing still.

This was nerve-racking; we knew not to expect any sort of signal telling us to "buy now," so we had to wait patiently and stay tuned into the market as best we could. Again, I feel compelled to highlight that we had no advanced statistics, reports indicating REO listing growth, or any outside data other than our daily review of what was on the market via the MLS. I keep bringing this up because I think it is vital for all full-time employees to know that you can start and finish a journey that ends in financial independence, even while you work your day job and without any special access to insider information.

While the market continued to fall, we started to notice a reduction in price drops. Instead of falling by $10,000 every 30 days, they started to fall by just one or two thousand. We also noticed a few of the "star" properties we identified would sell inside of 30 days. Upon identifying these signs of an impending upturn, we felt it was time to make offers and invest in REOs.

What? Banks Aren't Lending to Me!

Despite what seemed like a breakthrough, our world became even more frustrating once we started making offers. We were finding deals better than we had ever seen, and we had a track record of successful investments. In fact, we had avoided most of the pain of the downturn by moving all of our equity into small apartment buildings with in a year of the peak.

Unfortunately, we were about to encounter our first new reality of this negative market. As it turned out, banks did not want to grant loans on investment properties. Sure, they talked a good game, but based on our experience, one would think that the banks perceived investors as incompetent, fiscally irresponsible goons—including the ones who escaped the downturn relatively unharmed. It was incredibly frustrating.

Since we had good credit, plenty of income, and a track record documented via tax returns, we were accustomed to getting loans processed and completed inside of 45 days. Now we had to suffer through a 60-day process to secure the smallest real estate loan we ever needed. The low price point seemingly didn't matter, and we had to switch banks halfway through the process. After a lot of frustration and stress, we successfully acquired a bank loan and two additional properties for our portfolio. One was a four-bedroom two-bath house, and the other was quality duplex.

After completing the second bank loan, we were essentially told that there was no chance we would get another, because our net worth was all in real estate and we were seen as a bad risk. We felt horrible. The market was the best we would ever see in our careers, and to be blocked from it just when we were jumping back in was devastating.

It was clear that we needed to find a different way to fund our deals. We had no idea how to accomplish this, and we felt stuck once again.

The Four-Loan Limit

As we were fighting our disappointment, we started to learn about some of the artificial rules being put in place by banks and financial institutions. The one that hurt us the most was the rule that any one investor could only have four real estate loans. It didn't matter how much reserve you had, or how small your down payment would be. If you had four real estate loans (including any loans on your primary residence), no bank would be willing to make a fifth loan.

How could this be?

I suppose you have to appreciate the lenders' pain. During the downturn, they had made many loans to investors who kept pyramiding their debt, and when it finally broke, the investor lost it

Michael Zuber – *Financial Freedom One Rental at a Time*

all. Lenders were routinely dealing with individuals who were defaulting on five or more properties at a time.

I can understand the lenders' logic. Given these circumstances, it's not a leap to predict that an investor with five or more properties is likely to default, but an investor with four or less properties may be able stick it out until the market recovers.

While I understand this sentiment, I believe it actually caused the bottom of the market to form deeper and farther away than it had to be.

As an investor, I can tell you that the only folks I saw even glance at the real estate market during this time were well-seasoned and experienced. All the newbies and small-time players were either washed out or holding on tight to the little they had while the market got progressively worse.

And due to how bad an investment real estate was generally perceived to be, there also weren't any new investors stepping in. I believe the market fell further than it had to because the supply of buyers was greatly restricted, and the few that wanted to buy couldn't because the banks cut them off at four loans.

It was the classic mistake of the powers-that-be using the past and very real facts to drive future decisions, not realizing the market had drastically changed and that banks needed experienced investors to step in. Unfortunately this did not happen, and lending stayed tight for a long time.

67

As prices continued to decrease and supply increased, it finally happened: the bottom appeared. It turned out that big, well-funded hedge funds saw a ripe opportunity to prosper. They came in hard, and bought everything that wasn't nailed down. Just like our research indicated, the bottom appeared quickly and suddenly.

I never researched the hedge funds' business plans, but this is my guess: they planned to swoop in and buy with cash. They would repair units with cash and rent them out.

After two to three years, they would refi their portfolios and extract at least 150% of the cash they invested. After another two or three years, they would take their portfolios public via a company or REIT, thus extracting 200% or more profit.

It was a genius move, and let's face it, they had the cash available in a world where the well of bank financing had dried up. Plus, they could hold out for a few years until the financing market righted itself, and then extract all of their initial cash and then some. They know that investors have eight-year memories, so they will eventually take these investments public and profit again. Again, this is just a guess. I don't know anyone running a fund, but it does make logical sense to me.

REO Agents

As a fedgling investor, I remember reading a lot about REO Agents. I knew what the acronym stood for (Real Estate Owned), but

I could never find one when I first started. The reason for this became obvious to me only after living through the downturn.

When I first started investing, the market was in a clear up-cycle and Fresno was hot, so anyone who needed to sell was able to. If you bought a property six months earlier and needed to raise capital, there was every chance you would be able to get all of your cash back, pay the transaction cost, and squeeze out a profit.

There is little necessity for an REO in an upward market, and there were likely no full-time REO agents at that time. Sellers who needed to sell just had to list their property and boom, they had an offer inside of two weeks.

However, something became very clear during the crash. A handful of agents were getting the lion's share of the listings and they were insanely busy. Every investor was calling them up for data or trying to push for this or that deal.

Quality REO agents actually started setting up teams to filter out investor calls, as they couldn't keep up with all the people making promises and not closing.

The individual REO agents were making a good living but their relationships with their banks were precarious, as they knew their bank could yank future listings and give them to someone else. This reality meant REO agents were very focused on making the banks happy.

The banks' needs were pretty simple. They wanted to open and close escrows as quickly as possible, since every house they took back was a liability. There were break-ins and squatters causing property damage and all types of problems for the increasing number of empty houses.

Understanding that the REO agent's number one goal was closing all deals in escrow became our secret to acquiring more deals. We had heard REO agents talk about 50% failure rates and their fear of losing the stream of income from REO listings.

When we figured this out, we made it a point to get to the top REO agents in our market and establish ourselves as trusted buyers who always closed. I am happy to report that we closed 100% of the deals we put in escrow during the REO wave. Even though a few of our properties came with extra "surprises," we knew it was better to keep a perfect closing streak than to ask for a $1,000 credit for a broken window.

Once REO teams and agents knew we would close on any property we put in escrow, they started bringing us "problem properties" to consider. Some of these were too problematic for us to buy, which we would tell them up front and within 24 hours of their proposal. This is important; REO agents deserve timely answers you can stand by, and they got that from us every time.

Our main takeaway from this experience was that if you ever encounter a situation in which a handful of agents control a ton of listings, it would be a good idea to find out what motivates them and then see what you can do to help them. The relationships we created with REO agents during the downturn added a ton of value to our real estate portfolio, and really set us up to retire when we were ready.

Buying Foreclosures

As with REO agents, I had read numerous articles about buying foreclosures, but I never actually saw a property foreclose until the market turned. Then for a while it seemed like foreclosures were the only things on the market. Who would want to compete with the declining price points being established month after month?

I don't know if our experience here is typical, but again, I am here to share our specific experiences.

A few things stood out about buying foreclosures.

Response Time to Offers

The process of buying a foreclosure starts no differently than that of a regular property— with writing an offer and submitting it to the listing agent. What seemed to vary from offer to offer was the agent's response time, regardless of what you put in the offer. It could take them anywhere between 24 hours and several weeks, as the banks had their own process they had to go through. It was clear from the beginning that no standardized process existed, as some offers were immediately accepted and others were countered at the original asking price. Sometimes it took a day, and a few times it took weeks to get a response.

Banks were not motivated by time; they had checks and balances to run through, not to mention daily waves of inventory that needed attention. I'm sure it had to be a very interesting time to be in the banking industry.

End-of-Month Pressure

Buying foreclosures also led us to experience end-of-month pressure. This was never verbally confirmed by an REO agent or bank, but I can tell you our success rate on offers seemed to spike the closer we got to the end of each month.

I suspect this had to do with some kind of monthly financial reporting. Some banks were probably trying to manage to a certain number of purchases were therefore very eager to accept offers on the last few days of the month if it meant they would meet their quota.

As I discussed very early on, it pays to stay engaged in your market, and you will eventually pick up on little subtleties that will help you along the way.

Empty Properties

Walking into a bank-owned property was always interesting; you never knew what you were going to see. It could be a beautiful house that was nearly rent-ready, or a disaster area with squatters who had kicked in the back door and hosted a raging party the night before. We walked into at least fifty houses in the middle of the afternoon to find someone sleeping on the floor.

As we kept buying REO properties, we would perform our walkthroughs between 1:00 and 4:00 PM in order to avoid surprising anyone who might be squatting. We also liked to take advantage of the daylight rather than depending on flashlights for visibility.

Something about a vacant home always felt sad to us, knowing it had recently housed a family and was now sitting empty, just waiting to be brought back to life. I was very proud of the fact that we were able to help revive these homes by investing in them, applying a new coat of paint, boosting their curb appeal, and eventually turning them into quality housing.

Dual Commission

During the peak of distress in the real estate market, we decided to cut out the middleman and deal with listing agents directly. This was faster and our chances of receiving an acceptance were far greater.

We would find a property listing, do our homework, and call the listing agent with the amount we were willing to offer. If the agent liked the offer, we asked them to write it up. If they did not, we would either counter or assure them we were experienced investors actively buying properties. Most importantly, we would tell them that we closed 100% of the properties we got into escrow and we were happy to share names to validate this claim.

I am sure the dual commission helped us, but as I shared before, I believe many of the phone calls we received about shaky escrows were due to the fact that agents could count on us closing.

I remember getting a call from an agent saying their buyer was getting flaky, and they feared the bank would blame them and potentially revoke any future listings from them. The agent was flustered and wanted to know if we were game to make a backup offer. We did make an offer after collecting the details, and added the kicker that we would close in ten days or the bank could keep our deposit.

The agent thanked us profusely and subsequently brought us additional listings to consider, all because of the fact that we were able to close everything we had in escrow. Funnily enough, the buyer ended up closing and our backup offer was never used, but the agent knew we supported them and that we would have closed if required.

Reputation Matters

As outlined in the above story, while the REO market was picking up speed, the most important thing was not the offer price. Rather, it was one's reputation for closing deals.

We understood this from the start, and as we continued to close on properties, we received an increasing number of phone calls about troubled escrows and buyers backing out last minute.

Of the last fifteen or so REOs we bought, all but one of them were properties that someone else had locked up first but were unable to close. Being a buyer with a perfect record for closing was a huge asset, and one that added to our portfolio and cash flow every month.

A Common Foreclosure Repair

After we had bought ten or so REOs, I started to notice an expensive problem. Most REOs had been vacant for at least six months by the time we bought them. This meant that the trees in the area had no water from sprinklers, and therefore did what they could to survive. In most cases that meant their roots would work their way into the pipes of the house to reach whatever water was there.

When we would eventually turn the house and rent it to a nice family, the trees and their roots would soak up a bunch of water from the pipes. Guess what happened next?

You guessed it! The roots expanded and water pipes cracked. I think we had to replace six water lines out of the first ten properties we bought within thirty days of moving in a tenant. Shockingly, it costs a lot of money to dig out and replace a broken pipe.

The optimist in me started to see these events as signs that we were doing good work. We wanted the house and everything around it to thrive—even the darn trees.

Online Bank Sites for REOs

The last topic I want to highlight in regards to foreclosure is something that I saw take effect near the end of the cycle. It appeared to me the banks thought selling REOs was easy, and in an attempt to cut out the middleman, started posting their own listings.

As with many misguided efforts to make real estate more profitable, it didn't work. I understand the base logic, but because these bankers were out of state in most cases, they had no idea what they were doing.

Some banks would only accept full price offers and kick everything back, never stopping to listen to you justify your offer. In fact, many of them would become visibly annoyed even when a low offer was clearly appropriate because the house had been broken into, the front door was missing, or it had sustained some other form of property damage that would lower the value of the building.

We successfully bought one or two properties from bank REO sites. However, it is our experience that the banks actually netted less money and took a lot more time to close, as both escrows took nearly sixty days through no fault of our own. It just took them that long to get paperwork together.

Again, I understand the logic the banks were using when they thought the applications were a good idea, but my personal experience is that they extended time frames, added risk, and failed to net more money across their portfolio of REOs.

Replacement Cost

Until the market crash, I had never really understood the concept of replacement cost.

It made sense to me on some level because each of the properties we owned needed to be insured for a replacement cost, but the numbers never really stuck with me until we started to buy properties at prices far below said cost.

I remember the first time we bought a property for about $50,000. The replacement cost as indicated on our insurance paperwork was over $150,000. I actually called our insurance broker to ask what was going on. We had just paid a third of that for the house, so why was the replacement cost so high?

His answer stuck with me. He said, "Congratulations, you just bought a property for thirty percent of the cost to build it from scratch!"

While the REO cycle was in full flight we bought dozens of properties significantly below replacement cost, which meant we would see a natural rise in value as the market healed itself.

We didn't know how long this would take, but we believed property values had to bounce back to their original replacement costs or we would never build a new house again. We had no idea how long this would take, so we just kept on buying properties.

What You Can Do When Banks Say "No"

As I mentioned earlier, we were told at the start of the REO cycle that due to the four-loan limit, banks would no longer lend to us. We were cut off, and we had to reassess our plan and come up with a way to keep buying in the best market we had seen to date.

We had the option to pay cash for investments, which would work but it would a slow process. We estimated that we might get two or three great properties during the whole cycle if we went this way.

We could try credit unions, other banks, and mortgage brokers. We called around, but the story was the same. We were the enemy (read: risky) and none of them wanted to lend to us.

Lastly, we thought to find types of lenders other than traditional banks. We were very fortunate to establish a relationship with a local hard money lender. This relationship empowered us to buy a property a month for over a year.

Hard Money Lenders

I don't know the official definition of a "hard money lender," but in my experience, the hard money lender has the ability to make loan decisions by themselves. They likely have a framework and fee structure that may seem expensive until you realize they are helping you buy many distressed assets quickly. They can fund in record time, requiring only a clean title and some signed documents.

In our case, we found a hard money lender relationship that allowed us to put down only 30% of the purchase price, asked for three points up front, and charged 9% interest on the borrowed money. All of these variables were much higher than we were used to, but again, it was our only option in terms of financing.

We were sure to share our plan with the lender, as we didn't want to be a "one and done" borrower. We wanted him to know that we planned to be back, and we wanted to know with confidence that we had a "yes" answer every time.

He was very professional and really helped us frame our plan. It was hugely beneficial to work with someone who had been dealing with real estate investors for years and had seen up and down cycles before. To this day, he is a trusted financial resource and friend of the family. We still have several loans with him and we would not be where we are today without his tremendous resources and support as we continued to add REOs to our portfolio.

Understanding Yield vs. Cash Flow

It was during one of our many conversations with him that the notion of "yield" popped into my head. We were reviewing the expected numbers on a few of our latest investments when he pointed out that we had a 15% yield on a particular property. I knew it was a good deal but I had never looked at it that way before. I was so fixated on cash flow that nothing else mattered.

As he walked me through the math to reveal the 15% yield, it was like seeing a rainbow and unicorn at the same time. It was magical, and I would never look at a real estate property the same way again. Every property since then has been a "yield play" rather than a "cash flow."

Our lender indicated that if you put up, say, $20,000 and expect to earn $3,000 a year in net cash flow every year going forward, the property was producing a 15% yield. 3,000/20,000 = .15 * 100% = 15%.

From this conversation onward, I completely pivoted on our future investments and used yield to rank properties instead of expected cash flow. This simple tweak meant I would be less likely to take on a huge make-ready cost—cash that might be better served buying a cleaner property at slightly higher price. This pivot led me to conserve cash and only deploy it when it would maximize my yield.

In other words, I made sure each dollar I put into an investment was working hard for me.

Private Money

"Private money" and "hard money" appear to be similar concepts, but are actually very different. Please know that there are plenty of rules and regulations on private money, so please research them before taking any action. I wanted to share our story without going into too much intricate detail that would be better covered by experts.

In dealing with both hard and private money, there is no bank involved, the terms are generally higher than those of a bank, and you will be making payments over a defined timeframe.

The key difference in our case was that friends and family started to approach us, offering to loan us money. It was our hard money lender who suggested we take them up on the offer, given the high rate of return and security we could offer them—not to mention the fact that we would save on fees and expenses.

We will outline our private money loan process in the next section. It was critical to us to provide the most security possible to our friends and family. We almost wanted them to hope we forgot to pay them so they could foreclose on us and end up ahead of the game.

Our base structure was a 10% interest payment for 10 years, which our friends and family were excited about. At the time, they were earning less than 1% from the bank. As you will see in a minute, we not only paid a high interest rate for private money loans, but we ensured they had the utmost security. It was also important to us to be able to extract most of our capital and keep it moving to the next purchase.

Four Steps: Buy, Repair, Lease, Finance

We probably didn't have to set up the following private money loan structure, but we wanted our friends and family to feel completely comfortable lending to us, so we created this four-step process that we executed over and over again.

1. We would buy a property for cash and 100% our money.

2. We would then repair the unit with our capital.

3. We would lease the property and move a tenant into our newly renovated unit.

4. At this point we would go to our private lender ("The Bank of Friends and Family") and establish a loan that allowed us at least a 90% return of capital (if not 100%). We would pay 10% interest only and file all the paperwork ensuring that the lender could easily foreclose and take back the property if we didn't pay. We would sign a note and a deed of trust just like we would with a bank loan.

This simple four-step process made us feel really good, was greatly appreciated by our friends and family, and best of all, allowed us to continue to reuse capital over and over again. Like an assembly line, we had one or two projects in flight at all times for nearly two years.

The process helped us add a lot of great properties to our portfolio, and we would not have been financially independent without it.

Buying Distressed Multi-Unit Apartment Buildings

As you read earlier in our story, we began investing in single-family homes before moving to small multi-unit buildings as housing prices increased.

Guess what? It happened again. As competition in the single-family market started to heat up, we began looking around for other investment options. We didn't like the way the market was going; something felt different and we couldn't put our finger on it.

When the single-family market got to competitive we simply started looking at the small multifamily market. We had never seen an REO on an apartment building, and we were not sure how that would happen given the security offered in traditional commercial loans. However, downturns can wipe out a lot of solid investments, including small apartment buildings.

At the tail end of the REO cycle, we found two 10-unit buildings and one 18-unit building in the process of being foreclosed. As with the different lending requirements I highlighted in our second phase, the REO process was vastly different with regard to apartment buildings.

Most importantly, banks that held troubled loans were very interested in talking with potential buyers who had long track records of buying distressed assets.

This bank in particular was interested in writing a loan that required very little down payment, and they were willing to waive various fees in order to get a trusted investor to take over the property and start paying back the loan.

Each of these three small buildings were negotiated directly with the bank inside of a week, and all we had to do was send weekly progress reports and pictures of the improvements we made in the first ninety days. With these final three properties, we had completed 90% of our acquisitions during the real estate crash.

We had gone from owning around 65 units to owning 175 units in the span of four years, and we were ready to let the properties season themselves, settle down, and see what we really earned after all the activity.

My Mantra During the Downturn

I had one mantra that I kept repeating to myself during the real estate crash: I don't want to be that guy who says, "I wish I bought more." I can't tell you how many books I read in which the writer admitted regretting not buying more properties during the downturn.

I was desperate not to utter those words in the future. I can only think of one additional 10-unit building that I tried to secure but ultimately relinquished to a family friend. I might have been able to squeeze it into the portfolio, but my capital would have been very tight and I wouldn't have been able to do the remodel in the right way, so I gave the listing to a friend and he did an outstanding job turning the eyesore into a beautiful property.

Other than that one building, I'm happy to say we bought everything we could and I don't regret missing any opportunities.

Hedge Funds Enter the Market

As mentioned previously, we knew something was different in the single-family market, and this shift became obvious months later when big-money hedge funds started entering the market and buying properties right out of the MLS. These hedge funds were writing offers on properties without looking at them, confirming our hunch that a bottom was being put in the market at the tail end of our single-family acquisition—and the good times were all but over.

When big money players want in, they come in hard and push out all the little guys. They soak up all the supply and become the giant buyer all agents want to deal with. Where we had previously been receiving a phone call or two a week regarding available properties, we were getting zero now, as real estate agents were getting both sides of the commission and preferred to deal with the same buyers repeatedly.

We saw the bottom of the market coming because we were paying attention every day and putting little indicators together to predict likely outcomes. We didn't know exactly why things were changing, but our offers were not being accepted, listings were locked up before we could call on them, and the quality of available listings took a huge hit, since all the good properties never even made it to the MLS once the hedge fund buyers showed up. The hedge funds snagged all the pocket listings and they laughed all the way to the bank, leaving the small investors to wonder what had happened.

The Media Finally Turns Positive

The real estate market seemed hopeless for five years straight. Then a shift occurred. Real estate articles started to take on a slightly less apocalyptic tone. Later, a few more articles were downright positive, and pretty soon, the market was off the bottom. I started to see articles written about price growth, increasing demand, and new loan programs.

I believe that people generally want to read about positive news, and after hitting the bottom, I predict that real estate will enjoy a ten- to twelve-year run of it. Because investors seem to have eight-year memories, this will lead to the next real estate cycle and new investors thinking the market will never go down.

It is my hope that we don't compound this excitement with ridiculous loan options and disgraceful lending standards that add gasoline to the upside. I have lived through several market cycles, and the downside is brutal. I hope nothing like the 2008 market crash happens again, but if it does, do ensure that you will be ready and keeping a close eye on the market.

Market Begins to Heal Itself

Once the hedge funds entered the game, inventory started to dry up. Next came the encouraging articles, and lo and behold, the market started to heal itself. In fact, as of this writing I believe the market is now on year six of price appreciation. Lending is by no means easy, but it is certainly more accessible than it was at the peak of the stress.

Like the other real estate cycles I researched and referenced earlier, the Fresno market was healing itself and putting in the framework for sustained and healthy growth.

Deal in Review

In this chapter, I wanted to review the second 10-unit building we secured near the tail end of the real estate crash. We had bought the first building directly from an owner who agreed to finance the building at 100% as long as we put $30,000 in an escrow account for repairs.

While that story is interesting, I want to talk about the building next door, which turned out to be a foreclosure owned by a small local bank. The bank president was taking regular trips to review the building, and he was not happy with what he saw. The building was getting worse and he felt stuck.

That is when he saw my team working on our 10-unit building next door. While his building had tenants, mine was vacant, and he could see all the lucrative investments we were making in the building. He came by several times over the next couple of weeks to make sure we were not some flash-in-the-pan investors before asking for the owners' contact details in hopes of making us an offer.

During our phone call he indicated that he was interested in selling his building to an experienced investor. He wanted to meet us to discuss our full portfolio and our thoughts on his building.

We met the following weekend and discussed what we had done over the last fifteen years— most importantly, all the properties we had bought and brought back to life. He was impressed and asked us what it would take for us to buy his building.

After some additional fact-finding, we agreed to purchase the property for the outstanding loan balance so he wouldn't take a loss if he financed the property at 100% and we wouldn't have to bring any money to closing. He even gave us half a percent off the mortgage rate because we were doing him a huge favor. Just like that, we had another 10-unit building, and this time it was 100% financed by the bank.

I fundamentally believe that, as demonstrated by these two examples, single-family homes and small apartment markets run in completely different cycles that are not synced up at all. It is these different market cycles that have allowed us to jump out of one hot market and into a less competitive one on multiple occasions.

Phase 4: Hit the Pause Button

After nearly four years of rapid acquisitions, it was once again time to hit the pause button on our investments. Our portfolio had more than doubled, and we needed to take stock.

The fact is, we were running so hard and so fast during the real estate crash that we never reviewed our portfolio; we were solely focused on closing our next deal. We never wanted to feel like we left money on the table, and we just kept hunting for deals.

When the hedge funds and big money players started making offers on MLS listings, we took it as a signal to take a breather and repeat the acquisition hiatus that had worked so well for us earlier.

We were happy with all our acquisitions, but now it was time to manage the portfolio that peaked at over 175 "doors" (in other words, 175 tenants paying rent checks). That's a lot of tenants, and we wanted to take a break to just manage this portfolio for a while. We had been so busy running our assembly line of "buy, repair, lease, and finance" that we had ignored some basic management of our portfolio.

We spent several months reviewing each property to make sure there was no deferred maintenance that should be done, and that we were maximizing rent. Once we started to tier our properties, it became clear that some were long-term keepers and others weren't.

Take Stock

During our break, we also found ourselves taking stock of where we were in our journey towards our ultimate goal of financial independence.

It had been about nearly fourteen years and we had never stopped to reflect back on our investment career. We were always looking ahead, which I now feel was a huge mistake. We should have taken time to enjoy the process a little, but I guess when I latch onto a goal I don't let go.

I now recommend all investors review their progress every year. It's a long journey, but you will get there one year at a time. We never did this, and constantly looking ahead to the next deal proved to be very stressful and not as fun as it should have been. We should have celebrated more, and were unaware that the process didn't have to feel like work all the time.

Real estate investing is not easy, and challenges lie around every corner. I believe that this would have been much less stressful if we simply stepped back every now and again to discuss our portfolio.

Olivia Quits Her Day Job

One thing we realized during our second break was that if we stopped buying properties and performing required make-ready costs in REOs, we would actually have a very healthy monthly cash flow. This might sound odd, but when you have a full-time job that takes you all over the world and you are buying properties as fast as you can, you might not thoroughly parse the numbers and realize the distinction between one-time make-ready costs versus normal monthly expenses.

To be clear, we knew that since we had not been dipping into our personal accounts to fund our acquisition binges, we were cash flow positive every month, but we had no real idea how significant the positive cash flow actually was. As our pause in acquisitions hit ninety days, it became clear that we had established a portfolio that was producing tens of thousands of dollars in monthly cash flow.

This fact was only reaffirmed as we watched our portfolio for another ninety days to confirm our findings. Please know we had spreadsheet calculations and lots of theories regarding our cash flow, but nothing beats actual experience and hard facts. When we saw another three months roll by with large chunks of positive cash flow, we looked at each other and said the magic words that we had been dreaming about:

"Honey, you can quit your job!"

We had our monthly expenses covered and then some. With that, Olivia retired and she has never looked back. She has taken up painting, volunteering, and just doing whatever she wants to do.

I have to admit that setting a goal of retirement and financial freedom is one thing, but making our way through a long journey that included an artificial peak and a devastating crash is something I will always be proud of. We could have been crushed dozens of times by market forces, and we not only beat them but were able to use them to our advantage.

Did I Leave My Job Too?

The short answer is no, I did not leave my paycheck job at the same time as my partner—for a couple of reasons.

We were risk averse, and while we had a track record of cash flow that paid all our bills, we wanted extra evidence that we were financially secure. We agreed that I wouldn't even consider retirement unless we went another twelve months successfully living solely on our real estate income.

The second reason may seem silly, but I loved my day job and would have done it for half my salary. I worked in a fast-paced software company where I was the leader of a team of the best and brightest people tackling huge challenges and we were exceeding expectations. I find no greater thrill than leading and inspiring people to take on challenges that they did not think were possible.

However, after watching my wife thoroughly enjoy her retirement for four years, I was left with a nagging question. Sure I loved my job, but it took me all over the world and consumed so much of my time and energy. I wasn't getting any younger; could I do something else and be just as happy, more balanced even?

This question really ate at me. I still had that passion for my day job, but I couldn't help but wonder what would happen if I left it for something entirely different and less taxing.

As I type this, I know two things for certain.

First, I retired from my day job in March of 2018, and now I need to see if I can make the mental shift to not working a day job. It is harder than you think when you love your job, you are the best at it, and you make a decent income.

Second, I need to focus on real estate and helping people, or I will just end up going to a different software organization. I need to be busy, and I want to help people do great things.

All things considered, it makes the most sense to me to get my real estate agents license. This would allow me to help other full-time employees invest in buy-and-hold real estate. Who knows if this will work out? I may even open my own brokerage! Now that I have the time, I am also considering establishing a fund with friends and family to execute short-term flips.

In the end, I want to challenge myself. We worked a long time for one goal, and now that we have achieved it, I want to see if I can find a new passion. It is entirely possible that in a few months I will say "Nope, I need the structure and challenge of a day job; time to go back to work!"

Again I don't know how this will turn out, but I must say having options is such a great feeling, and I owe it to myself to see if I can help others start on their own path to financial freedom.

What Do You Want Your Life to Stand for?

As I stand on the precipice of retirement, this is the question that haunts me. I have defined myself as a successful and inspirational leader for over two decades now, and I don't know anything else.

I know I can't play golf every day, and going to the gym only takes an hour or so. How am I going to fill the rest of my days? I am still young, and I have too much energy and passion left to do nothing.

As stated above, I am fully aware that I may jump back into a full-time job. The difference is that if I do it will be because I *want* to, not because I *have* to. However, I am going to try and refocus my passion and energy on helping others achieve financial independence. The best part of my day job has always been helping and inspiring people to do great things, and I am going to try and do that outside the confines of W2 employment.

Frankly, this book is my first step in giving back. I can remember looking through Amazon, hoping to find a real estate investor's complete end-to-end story of becoming a successful buy-and-hold investor. I never found one, and I am writing this to fix that; it is absolutely possible to use buy-and-hold real estate to establish financial freedom.

Helping people understand the ins and outs of buy-and-hold real estate investing is my new goal, and my hope is that it becomes my daily source of excitement and passion.

Do We Rebalance Our Portfolio?

As I join Olivia in retirement, we are left with a few choices to make. Do we keep the portfolio as-is? Should we prune just a few properties and keep most of them? Are we going to get radical and sell off the apartment buildings, pay off the houses, and live debt free?

It is nice to have options, and while I strongly suspect we will sell off a few properties, I am unsure if we even want to sell our apartments and use the proceeds to pay off all our debt. It is a question we are currently wrestling with, and I am not sure which way we will go.

On one hand, removing all debt from the equation is an interesting option to consider. On the other hand, having a large base of rentals means that our portfolio will increase in value while properties continue to rise in the near future.

Paying Off Rentals

This next bit might seem obvious, but I don't want to leave any stone unturned in this book. On our journey to financial independence, it was never our goal to pay off our properties. Shoot, we were so busy saving for the next deposit that paying off a property was the furthest thing from our minds. However, now that we are finally former employees, one of our options is to sell our apartments and pay off all our houses.

It might sound strange, but having no debt on our remaining properties means we get extra cash flow every month, as we are not peeling off a certain percentage to the banks. However, given our belief that real estate is currently in a nice appreciation phase, we might want to sit tight and let inflation raise the value of our properties.

My prediction is that we will agree to sell one or two buildings, build a nice financial cushion, and pay off a dozen properties. Regardless of what we do, it is nice to have options.

What to Keep

Our current portfolio is made up of:

3 – 18-Unit Buildings

1 – 13-Unit Building

4 – 10-Unit Buildings

1 – 7-Unit Building

2 – 5-Unit Buildings

2 – Triplexes

6 – Duplexes

35 – Single-Family Homes

Considering all of the options and variables, it's difficult to decide what we should and shouldn't keep. For example, did you know that all commercial loans have fixed rate periods that end after five or ten years? If interest rates rise and we get a reset at the wrong time, that could hurt.

Did you know that single-family homes have the greatest variability, and should another storm hit in the future, the single-family market will get hit the hardest?

How about decisions that should be easy? One might think it's obvious to keep properties located in the best areas and sell the "bad" ones. Well, who is to distinguish a "bad" area from a "good" one? Some so-called "bad" areas are great locations for investments, and a few seemingly nice areas actually have high rental turnover rates, as tenants become owners when they find what they are looking for.

In the end, should we consolidate? I suspect we will likely let go of one or two 18-unit buildings and maybe one or two houses that have not met our cash flow expectations over several years.

What's Next?

Good question. First things first—I've always wanted to document our story, so I'm writing this book! If it helps just one person start their journey to financial independence, it will be worth it.

I suspect we will also do something in real estate on a more permanent basis, such as getting my real estate salesperson license. Over the years, I have helped put $10 million in deals together for other agents, so I wonder what I could do if I focused on this full time.

Maybe I will even go on a speaking tour. Shoot, maybe I will get bored and return to the job market for a few more years. Note that in this case I wouldn't have to work for someone else, and instead I would work on what I choose to work on, when I choose to do it. In the end, I am going to take some time off to see if I can make being retired work for me.

Employee Mindset

I must admit that I still fall victim to what I call the "employee mindset." You know, the little voice that demands that you get a job and claims that you are way too young to retire. I have been working at least one job since I was twelve, so I have spent over thirty years working for someone else. Walking out the door as an employee for the last time is harder than you would think.

Maybe I did this all wrong. Maybe I should have had a vacation or some other distraction planned when I got to the point of exiting my full time job. The fact is that I didn't, and now my employee mindset is playing tricks on me all the time.

I still freak out on occasion, but the ability to retire has been our goal for fifteen years. I know this is just a mental block that I need to get over, and I'm going to try to put together a life comprised entirely of my own choices until they put me in the ground.

What Can We Do to Help Others?

We have helped some families start buy-and-hold investment portfolios over the years. We have had friends who were interested in what we were doing and we'd bring them along on our regular trips to Fresno.

I bring this up because that feeling of helping others is incredibly rewarding. That feeling is what made my previous job worthwhile. I suspect I will need to somehow replicate that feeling during my retirement, or I am going to find myself back at a full-time job.

I will start out small by getting my real estate agent's license, but who knows where it might go from there. Maybe someday I will open a brokerage, or perhaps end up doing something entirely different. As I said before, it is nice to have options

What to Do When the Journey Is Over

It has taken us fifteen years to get where we are, and now that we are here, I must admit it is an odd feeling. Writing the opening section of this book was very cathartic, as I had forgotten about all the tough choices we made along this journey.

We have discussed four unique and key phases in our journey, and have now reached our goal. We are finally standing on top of the mountain. We are tired, we are excited, and at least at the moment, we are looking for the next thing to do.

When you are wired to be an employee, it is harder than you would think to get out of your head and lead an independent lifestyle. I don't know what lies ahead for us, but we will take some time and see if we can't fill our days helping other families take steps to their own financial independence.

Part One of this book was our story from start to finish. My goal for the first section was to try and paint you a picture of the four phases of our fifteen years of buy-and-hold investing.

In Part Two, I am going to call out twenty-one suggestions I have for you based on questions I have collected over the years. While Part One centered on our story, Part Two is going to be more direct with items we deem to be very important.

You ready? Here we go.

21 Key Topics Every Investor Needs to Understand

Understanding Your "Why"

I believe the first thing you have to understand as you get ready to commit to a decades-long journey is *why* you want to do it. The "why" has to be specific, meaningful, and something you can lean on when things get hard, because they will.

The long voyage will not always go your way, and if your "why" does not hit you at your core, you may give up as soon as you hit a bump in the road.

Remember that first property we bought on Norris Drive? It delivered a big dose of pain immediately, and this could have knocked us off of our path before we even got started. Along the way, we've had plenty of other tenant issues, lost deals, and nasty surprises.

When things got bad, we reviewed and discussed our "why," dusted ourselves off, and kept moving forward. Any goal that takes decades to achieve will have negative surprises occur, and they might occur frequently.

So, what do I consider an incomplete "why?"

The most frequent "why" I hear goes something like this:

"I want to be financially free."

"I want to be rich."

"I want to retire"

"I want to quit my job."

All of these may sound good, and probably even feel good to say. However, I would say they are not meaningful enough. I believe someone who hears your "why" should be emotionally moved by it, or you are at best just skimming the surface.

A better "why" might be as follows:

"I want to be financially free in twenty years because I have seen how hard my grandparents had to work until the day they passed away."

"I want to be rich because I see all the injustices in the world and I want to give back to a cause that moves me."

"I want to be retired so I can coach baseball or tutor underprivileged kids."

"At the moment I do what I do only because it pays well and I don't feel like I have options, and I want to quit for peace of mind."

So I ask you: what is your reason for investing in real estate?

Please do me a favor and test your "why" with family and friends. Ask them if it feels rooted in genuine passion, or if it is just superficial. Your core reason for investing can evolve over time, but I believe it will stay fairly constant from start to finish.

Have Short- and Long-Term Goals

As I shared in the first half of this book, I failed to do the following and I don't want you to repeat my mistakes if I can help it. Specifically, I am referring to setting both short- and long-term goals and then celebrating when you reach them.

I decided years ago that real estate investing was going to be my path to financial freedom and I wasn't going to stop until I was done. Unfortunately, looking back on fifteen years of investing, this caused a problem. The journey is so long that daily life events can get in the way and distract, or worse, derail you from your end goal.

Having an end goal is great, but I see that as the top of the mountain, and I suggest you set up base camps along the way. No one should set a goal that will take decades to reach and climb without stopping. That is a mistake. Instead, I suggest breaking down goals into smaller chunks and treating them as base camps to review, reflect, and learn. From there, you can get going to the next base camp.

By establishing base camps, you can celebrate the small victories and feel great about getting to that point before starting on your way to the next goal.

Please do not repeat my mistake. Set small goals that take you to the end goal. For example, consider celebrating your first purchase, the first time you receive greater than $1,000 a month in positive cash flow, or the first time you buy a multi-family.

In the end, you are on a long climb to your end goal. Take care to celebrate the small victories, as they will be the energy you need to keep you going.

Get Buy-In

I believe the most important thing to do after pinpointing your "Big Why" is to get complete and certain buy-in from your significant other.

Please heed this advice. It is essential to sit down and talk to your significant other about why you want to do this. I strongly suggest that you also discuss all the potential bad things that may happen.

For example:

We will have months where we have a negative cash flow of several thousand dollars due to rental turn or a large repair.

We will need to sacrifice extras in our life to invest in this dream. That means we can't renovate the kitchen, we can't get a new car, and we can't take that nice vacation.

This will not be quick. It will take decades and it will feel like nothing is happening for years.

We will need to spend hours upon hours learning this business and looking at properties, and our taxes will be more complicated and more expensive.

Believe me when I say that you need to get all the bad stuff on the table and make sure everyone is ready before you start. The more buy-in and agreement you have before you invest a single dollar, the better off you will be. Investing in real estate is stressful enough; you don't need additional family stress.

Do Your Homework

As you read in Phase 2 of this book, I believe in doing your homework before making an offer on your first property. Most of this homework can be done online while you set up your foundation. You need to start to understand listings, inventory, and the basic trends of the market in which you are investing.

By reviewing online resources you can start to get a feel for new listings, pending listings, and properties that have been re-listed because another buyer backed out.

It is my belief that in order to research efficiently and maximize the return on your time, you need to think about limiting your search to a few zip codes. When I first started I would look at one particular zip code in an area of Fresno called the "Old Tower District," or 93728. This part of town happened to be older, close to downtown services, and full of long-term residences. There wasn't much new construction going on in the area, so my rentals were competing with older homes on the market.

I believe you should review at least fifty properties, build a spreadsheet, and start to get comfortable with what you know and what you don't know. For example, some information like listed bedrooms, square feet, and parking (garage, carport, street) is often readily available. You might even get a feel for the condition of the building based on photos. However, what you won't really know is the property's "make-ready cost," or how much it will cost to turn the unit into a quality rental. You won't know if there is an opportunity to create another bedroom (read: more rent) or any extra items that aren't included in the MLS description.

Once you have invested your time in basic research, I suggest trying to prioritize the homes from best to worst. Then I would take a few minutes to tell the story of the best ones and the worst ones to ensure you understand why they are good or bad investments.

Don't Buy or Create Alligators

I would like to once again reiterate the number one most important piece of advice in this book: whenever possible, do not ever buy or create alligator properties. To clarify, an alligator property is a building that eats personal cash from your pocket every month. As I shared in our personal story, I accidentally created an alligator property when I refinanced my first purchase to buy more property. In this instance I was lucky and the market kept appreciating, but you should never count on or plan for luck.

So again, never ever buy or create an alligator property. It is in fact much better to hold your cash than to buy an alligator. Now I realize I have no idea what market cycles might be like in the future, so let me say this:

If for some reason the market is high and the only properties available through standard financing seem to be alligators, you have two choices in my book.

You can stay engaged in the market and see what happens over time, with the knowledge that buying an alligator is never a good idea.

Or,

You can simply put down a larger down payment. Just because a bank will lend you 80% of the purchase price doesn't mean you have to accept it. Let's say your numbers show that unless you put 30% down, you will likely have an alligator on your hands. In this case, I would actually suggest putting down up to 40%, as I don't want you buying anything that could even come close to becoming a future alligator.

If it is not clear by now, I believe that buying, creating, and holding alligators will be the death of any investment career. Sure, you might buy one and hold onto it because you can afford the extra $200 it costs every month. You might even luck into 50% appreciation over a decade, but is that really worth it in the long haul?

My hope is that you have to foresight to realize that no, you cannot reach your long-term investment goals by having alligator properties in your portfolio. Don't do it!

Celebrate Small Victories

For most of my investment career, I neglected to celebrate the small victories, which I now realize was a huge mistake. As described above, the journey is long and full of potholes that try and throw you off track. I now believe that if I would have just taken a few moments here and there to celebrate, I would have found the process much more enjoyable.

My choice to keep my head down and never look back is not ideal, and almost wrecked our business on more than one occasion. See, when you neglect to celebrate accomplishments along the way, you forget about the good times as you suffer through the tough ones. Rough patches happen, and if you forget to remember the good times like your first positive cash flow or the first time you netted $1,000, these events can stop you in your tracks. Worse yet, you might just decide to sell everything and move on to something else.

Now when I say celebrate, I do not mean that you should go blow a bunch of money on a cruise or a new car; a celebration can be as simple as going out to dinner with a friend. The simple act of sharing your goodness with others will cost you very little, and will give you that little extra jolt of motivation while you remember the good times.

Please don't be like me and just go charging up the hill without looking back. It is not healthy and it is a lot riskier than taking time to celebrate the small victories.

Don't Sweat the Small Stuff

When you own a growing portfolio, have a full time job, and are responsible for family commitments, you become an extremely busy person. I strongly suggest that as your portfolio gets bigger, you try not to sweat the small stuff. For example, when our portfolio grew to around fifty units, we no longer required approval on any expense under $100. Up to that point, we were reviewing every expense with our team, which consumed a lot of time.

Once we established this new minimum on expenses, our need to approve and review items dropped by almost fifty percent. Before you ask, we did check in monthly on these to be sure no one was playing the system, but we were free from the daily burden of having to look at every expense.

Note that we had been working with our team for years by this point, and they knew how we operated. A side benefit to this was that our team got even stronger as they realized how much we trusted them to oversee our expenses. They did everything they could to support the trust that had been built over years.

I believe letting go of the small issues significantly reduced my stress level. You have no idea how stressed I would get when we had to go unclog a toilet or replace a light bulb for a Section 8 inspection. These things shouldn't have bothered me, but they did until I realized that I had to stop sweating the small stuff.

Personal Goals

While my personal goal all along has been to retire from my full-time job, this does not have to be your goal. Frankly, most of the investors I speak with don't yet see that as a real objective, and the idea frightens them a little.

Instead, I offer up two goals that might be better suited for you, as I believe having positive cash flow rentals is a good idea to balance ones portfolio.

My first suggestion is for families who either have kids or are planning to have kids.

I suggest aiming to acquire at least one positive cash flow unit per child to ensure you have a little extra nest egg available for when they go off to college, get married, or receive an inheritance. You may have already set up some type of savings account for your child, but a piece of real estate that serves as positive cash flow and appreciates at market rates means that you will have a nice chunk of change available should you need it.

My alternate suggestion is to consider a smaller end goal than retirement. Perhaps work toward replacing your primary income with real estate cash flow. Can you aim to cover the mortgage on your residence or car payment?

Regardless of your goal, I promise that you once you hit it you will set another. Remember to only buy positive cash flow properties, and when in doubt, either hold off or increase your down payment to ensure you have positive cash flow from the start.

My Favorite Metric

As with any market, there are a lot of metrics and esoteric terms thrown around in real estate. Rather than reviewing them one at a time, I will leave it to other books and the internet to define specific vocabulary. Instead, I want to talk about the one metric that I look at quarterly to reevaluate the market.

That metric is called the *affordability index*, and exists as an individual metric for any real estate market in which you are looking. I use this metric for several reasons, but most importantly, it highlights when the market is either getting overheated or is ripe for a bounce.

Let's say the affordability index is low—say, 15 percent. This means that only fifteen people out of 100 in Fresno can afford to buy the average house. Affordability is affected by lots of different variables that all work together.

The two most important variables are "average price" and "average interest rate." As either number rises, the cost of a house also increases. The other variable is "average income." It is possible that wages increase faster than the price of an average home in an inflationary environment, and thus affordability could in theory also increase.

I recommend taking a look at affordability in your market during, say, 2008, and then again in 2012. See a difference? What did it mean to buy in 2008 versus in 2012? Just for fun, try to figure out what the average rent was during those two years.

When the affordability in my market hits the teens, I get nervous and start looking for an exit. I don't usually sell and pocket cash, but I might sell and reposition equity into a small multifamily property. As I discussed earlier, repositioning equity was key to our long-term success in the last cycle.

Appreciate Market Cycles

Market cycles can help you or crush you if you do not appreciate them. Looking at other markets, I am convinced that most cycles differ in amplitude and duration. For example, one would say the market cycle in California is pretty severe in comparison to, say, that of Texas, which is considerably more gradual.

Note at which points during your market's cycle sellers have the power, and when buyers have the power. If you appreciate this shift alone, you will start to see how cycles can help you on your road to achieving whatever goals you set for your investments.

If you pay close attention to them you can use them over time to your benefit. As you saw earlier, we got lucky and were able to use two distinctly different portions of the market cycles to our benefit.

Please know you don't have to do this, and if you follow my rule of never buying or creating an alligator property, it won't matter what happens to prices in most cases.

Stay Engaged in Your Market

I highly recommend that you stay engaged in your market, and you should always be learning and observing its activity. If you only review the MLS when you have down payment money, you are sure to miss important details.

For example, you might have missed that the market in your area just flipped from a buyers' to a sellers' market. You might have missed the fact that low end of the market has exploded with interest, but the high-end units are not moving. You might have missed that one particular area is getting more interest because of big capital investments from the city or other outside forces.

Be sure to stay engaged in your market, as your most important lessons could come when you don't have any cash.

Review Your Progress

I think it is important to conduct an annual review because there are lessons to be had each and every year. I would suggest you *not* do this between Christmas and New Year's, because if you do, it will be glossed over by any other self-evaluation you do at year's end.

Instead, pick a day that means something to you, like a birthday or anniversary. I personally chose April 15 because, hey, it is tax day, and why not use it to think about your previous twelve months?

During this time of reflection, make sure to review the good and the bad of the previous year. Look for the lessons offered by each event. Ask yourself if there is anything you would do differently or what you will do next time in a similar situation.

In addition, make sure you review each property in detail to see how it performed. Look for areas of improvement, and if you find a surprise alligator, get rid of it. As you should remember by now, having or creating an alligator is never okay.

Bad Things Happen

I want to make sure everyone understands that while you can retire and achieve other financial goals with buy-and-hold rental properties, you'll face plenty of stressful situations along the way.

Remember that when you chose to be a landlord and to rent properties, you were taking on both the good and the bad side of the equation. You will need to understand and anticipate the unpleasant side because these things will happen when you own real estate as rental.

On the Physical Property Side:
- Items need to be maintained
- Items Break and need repair
- Items break and need to be replaced
- Roofs need to be replaced
- Water heaters break
- Leaks happen (small leaks to full-on floods)
- Fires happen

As a Landlord, You Will Have Tenant Challenges

- People won't pay
- People will lie
- People will vacate without notice
- People will rent as a couple and break up
- People will break things
- People don't always get along with neighbors
- People can get arrested
- People will die
- People will complain
- People will do all kinds of things

You are choosing to be a landlord, and that means you have additional risk from the properties you buy and the tenants to whom you rent. None of this should scare you away from being a landlord, but if it does, I am glad you know now before buying a rental and finding out the hard way.

Let me be clear: if any of the above scares you, I suggest looking for other investment options, as I have never seen a property where something didn't break and tenants didn't experience life events that affected their ability to pay rent.

Markets Change Suddenly

I don't know if the following is true, but I seem to recall reading something that said something along the lines of, "Your body is either growing or shrinking all the time, based on activity and diet."

Again, I don't know if this is true of human bodies, but what I can say for sure is this does apply to the real estate market, which is always evolving. While some may confidently distinguish between a "seller's market" or a "buyer's market," I can tell you I don't operate at absolutes like this.

I find real estate to be very local, down to the area or sometimes even street level, which is why I believe staying engaged in the market is so critical. I want to have the best data and information about my next investment, and not some report on national or even state statistics.

I do read and review national level statistics, but I do that so I can keep an eye on the larger story of real estate. I believe the purchase of first-time owner-occupied homes is greatly influenced by the national talk track on real estate. If the talking heads endorse investing in real estate, then first time-buyers have confidence, but if they say prices are falling, first-time buyers seem to disappear.

At the local level, what if you were looking at a cute little house that would be cash flow positive, only to find two weeks later that there are five new listings on the street? It might mean nothing, but it makes a lot of difference, as you are looking for cash flow positive properties. In this example, I would review all five listings and try and uncover the best property for cash flow or yield on required cash.

When you are investing in rental properties, you should prioritize your own numbers over any national or state statistics that highlight first time buyers or move up buyers. In most cases, those are not stats that should impact your decisions.

This Is a People Business

This is another topic that I didn't understand for years, and I hope you don't make the same mistake I did. Real estate investing is a people business. You will interact with dozens of people on any one transaction, not to mention all the folks you will work with once you own the property.

I entered the world of real estate investment with a decent head for numbers and a huge blind spot that could have cost me. In the beginning I was charging ahead like a socially inept bull in a china shop, which caused problems the longer I acted that way.

If you're in a people business and you lack social skills, people will just choose to work with other folks. Soon enough, you will be getting no deals.

I suggest that you appreciate this is a people business first, and do the small things right from the start. This can be as simple as sending a thank-you email or even a card to someone who helped you.

It never costs much to be nice, and the returns are large when you realize that almost no other investors go that extra mile. It seems many investors are like I was fifteen years ago, confident that their money was green and therefore people would happily work with them. That may be the case in a downturn, but when the market is hot, no one is going to choose to work with you, and you'll lose out on the best deals.

Do yourself a favor and learn from my mistake. Real estate is a people business, and you should act accordingly all the time.

Your Reputation Matters

Similarly, something you should hold in great regard is your own reputation, as it will become a factor that either attracts or repels deals.

I believe one of the key reasons I was able to secure so many properties during the real estate crash was that I had a reputation as a buyer who performed every time I got a property in escrow. Remember when the market crashed, which I discussed in Phase 3? That is the phase during which I learned that reputation matters.

If you are arrogant, disrespectful, or condescending to anyone in the real estate business, I promise you that word will get around. Here is the cold hard truth: regardless of how much money you have, no one *has* to deal with you. Worse yet, people may engage with you, but you will not be anyone's first priority. Not being at the top of someone's list is a problem, as real estate investment is a zero sum game.

If you are investing in real estate while holding down a full-time job, I promise you that your reputation matters even more, as you can't waste an opportunity to produce a cash flow property.

Look for Ways to Create Value

Once you have done your homework on a property, my hope is that you pick up on a few subtle things you can do to increase cash flow. Let me give you two examples of strategies I have used repeatedly.

Our first example has to do with increasing rent. Let's say we own a two-bedroom, one-bath house that rents for $1,000, and a three-bedroom, one-bath house that rents for $1,500.

Now what happens when you buy a 1,200-square-foot, two-bedroom, one-bath house that also has a living room and family room? In my experience, you will collect $1,000 a month, since bedrooms, bathrooms, and parking are the three greatest drivers of rent.

However, after walking through the house, you realize that the family room in the back of the house could become a bedroom if you closed off one wall and added a closet. Now there are rules regarding square footage, windows, etc., and you should check with your city or county to confirm you are always up to code, but you at least have the potential to create a three-bedroom.

I find this type of value creation to be particularly interesting when I can buy the property as a 2/1 and then rent it as a 3/1. The property's return will be higher because in general, two-bedroom houses are bought at a discount to three-bedroom houses.

The other option to create value is when you can work with the seller to structure a transaction that requires less down payment, as that will increase your yield (assuming you are still buying a cash flow property).

Remember: never buy or create an alligator! Never! To make myself extra clear, if an owner gave me a 100-unit apartment with zero down payment that was, say, a $500 a month alligator, I still would not buy it. This applies to every type of property, be it an apartment, house, or duplex. Never buy or create an alligator.

Anyway, back to my example. In a few cases I was able to work with the seller to finance the property. I sometimes achieved this with zero down, sometimes with 10% down, and a few times with just a large repair reserve held in escrow, if I was buying a distressed property that needed a lot of attention. When you can get a seller to carry the paper, you can save transaction costs with banks, negotiate interest rates, and discuss the terms of your contract. In these cases, use your creativity to create a win–win transaction that will benefit both parties.

You've Bought a Distressed Property—Now What?

You just brought a property that needs a lot of attention. What's next?

Well, after you build a general plan and take care of any urgent matters that could cause more damage—in other words, be sure to prioritize worker safety and the structural integrity of your building —I suggest you start outside.

Why outside?

Keep in mind that I am not a flipper but a buy-and-hold investor, and my intention is to place a tenant inside the unit once it is repaired. I find that dressing up the outside of a property first will lead potential tenants to stop by and ask questions, with the knowledge that the place is being renovated.

I did this exclusively during the real estate crash, and every single house was leased before we finished repairs. We got plenty of free marketing simply by addressing the front yard first. Please note that I am not talking about huge expense items like new grass, flower beds, or anything like that. Instead I am referring to more cost-effective approaches like mowing the grass, trimming the trees, power washing the exterior, and painting the trim.

I am also specifically referring to the front yard and any area that is visible as people walk or drive by. I wouldn't, for example, address the backyards of most properties until later, but the front yard should receive some attention right away.

In the end, if your plan is to lease or rent a property you just bought, I recommend that after addressing any critical items like roof leaks and broken windows, you start your improvements where potential tenants will easily see them. That is not in the kitchen or bathrooms, but outside in the front yard.

Did you know that most prospective tenants make up their mind when they drive by a rental house, regardless of how pretty the interior is? Again, you are in a people business, so start marketing to potential tenants by repairing the outside first.

Don't Touch Those Reserves

One issue I am sure you will encounter while you build a real estate portfolio is the push and pull of different seeming rules and theories. One of them is Murphy's Law as it applies to real estate: As soon as you have committed all of your capital, you are bound to find a great deal somewhere else.

When this happens, and it will happen, I am all for being creative and finding ways to buy the property. As I described earlier, I routinely borrowed from my 401K, and I was even open to getting a title loan on my car if I had to.

However, one place that is forever off-limits is your reserve fund for your real estate portfolio. I believe that you should never ever dip into this pile of money. I don't care if it is the deal of a lifetime and you only have ten days before you are liquid again. Don't do it.

Surprises happen, and your reserve fund is there to make sure you never lose the portfolio you already have. You should never risk it all for one more deal, regardless of how good it is. Are we clear? Never,

ever, dip into your reserve fund, but feel free to get creative and look for the money elsewhere.

Use Market Cycles to Your Advantage

I hope it is obvious by this point that we used the real estate market forces to our benefit. Specifically, there were three points in time over the last fifteen years that we took advantage of market forces.

As you may recall, we were buying solid rental units in the beginning, but as the market continued to rise, we felt stuck. We could either buy properties that didn't make sense with loan products we didn't trust (teaser loans); sit tight and see what would happen; or use the inflated market to our advantage and sell our single-family homes at prices we would never pay, and then 1031 Exchange the proceeds into small multi-unit buildings.

Our understanding that the market was telling us to be careful allowed us to save our equity in other buildings, increase our rent, and most importantly, increase our monthly cash flow.

I certainly hope we never see a market that is so out of balance again, but history says we will at some point in the future. If you have a few solid properties and see no way to buy more, then perhaps consider looking at a 1031 Exchange.

The second market cycle we saw is what most people refer to as "the real estate crash."

This is when a lot of loans went delinquent and short sales and REOs dominated the market. The slide started suddenly and violently, and for years the market kept falling. Demand disappeared, financing evaporated, and supply was exploding. This toxic mix of events meant that prices were falling fast, and if you could figure out a way to buy properties for cash, you could make some great progress.

We went the hard money route in the middle of this cycle, and later flipped to private money to continue buying. We bought everything we could, from single-family houses to an 18-unit apartment building. As I said earlier, I never wanted to be the guy who says, "I wish I had bought more."

Our final market force was the entry of hedge funds, which came in just as quickly and bought everything that wasn't nailed down. We stayed engaged in the market, but declining inventory meant prices were destined to rise, and that they did.

Prices have been increasing for years now, while supply is tight and demand is picking up. I suspect there is still a fair amount of room to go. Financing still seems to be difficult for investors, but so many other variables, like interest rates and recessions, can influence the market.

We are currently using this market cycle to reposition some debt, pay off some expensive loans, and look for other opportunities to reposition equity.

As market cycles go, it feels like we have gone full circle; I believe we are at the same point in the cycle when we started fifteen years ago. It was a great time to buy, and we wouldn't be financially free without those initial acquisitions that lead to 1031 Exchanges, and ultimately, the knowledge required to prosper during the real estate crash

Keep an Eye on REOs

My hope is that no real estate market ever suffers the violent drop in prices we saw during the crash again, as it hurt so many people. However, if market forces get out of control on the upside again, it will be a matter of not "if" but "when" the market will crash.

If you sense this may be happening, I suggest you sit back, stay engaged, and get ready to pounce in a huge way if the market turns as you expect. While we made money during every segment of the market cycle, the majority of our incredible monthly cash flow comes from assets we picked up at distressed prices during the crash.

So if REOs flood the market or supply again dwarfs demand by twenty to one, I suggest getting ready to add plenty of assets to your portfolio as quickly as possible. I know I will be out there with a huge shovel adding everything I can to our portfolio, since it is so easy to buy cash flow properties when no one wants them.

What Now?

I get this question a lot from friends and family. Since I was twelve years old I have had at least one job, and I have never taken a break from being an employee. Simply put, I loved every job I've had, as they each encouraged me to be creative, played to my competitive spirit, and allowed me to team up with great people.

I believe that I am going to spend the next few months trying to help one hundred people start their own journey. I suspect this will help replace that rush I got from loving my job and leading my teams to do amazing things.

After a couple days of decompressing and thinking about what I should do, I have decided to attempt the following:

1) I am going to help full-time employees see that buying "One Rental at a Time" can lead to financial freedom (now on www.onerentalatatime.com). I also have a YouTube channel by the same name——One Rental at a Time—where I discuss all kind of real estate investing topics.

2) I am going to get my real estate sales license, as it will give me more access to the market and allow me to help family and friends start their journey. My goal is to help one hundred investors a year start on their path to financial freedom.

3) If I enjoy being a real estate agent and helping new investors, I plan on also getting my brokers' license and opening a brokerage dedicated to investors.

4) I plan to use my knowledge of markets to add additional assets to our portfolio. This might be in the form of rentals or even flips, since I now have the time to research and manage flips. As discussed, flipping houses is a full-time job and not one I recommend for folks who already have demanding full-time jobs. If you do go for it, I wish you nothing but the best, as I never had the time or the energy to take on the task while I was working full time.

5) Lastly, I plan to create investing options for my friends and family that are secured by notes and first trust deeds. As you may remember, when the market was full of REOs, we established a program that paid 10% interest only for our family and friends. Now that the market is changing, I am designing an investment program that will allow them to receive a monthly interest rate, and most importantly, part of the profit. I am still working out the details, but I am calling it the "6 and 20 Program," and I suspect my family and friends will love this program just as much. Ideally they will receive a small interest rate and then 20% of the profit when the flip sells. I suspect hold times will be six to nine months, and therefore allow for quick and secure returns.

I don't know what the future holds, but I would also love to be interviewed on podcasts, radio shows and at real estate events. I would be excited to share our story to help full-time employees believe in the journey of buy-and-hold investing. It is a long path, but so worth it. If you know of a podcast, a real estate group, or real estate event that would like to hear from someone with fifteen-year history, please pass on my details.

Maybe the comfort of being an employee will drag me back into the workforce, but I don't think it will. I have had too much fun writing this book and thinking about future possibilities to give it up now!

All the best, and I hope this book has shown you that, yes, one rental at a time can lead to financial freedom and you don't have to be an employee forever.

My Journey After Retirement—One Year Later

I can hardly believe it myself, but it has been one year since I left the rat race. In this final section, I am going to walk you through my first year of retirement and share the good and the bad with you. Living without the demands of a full time job had some surprising downsides, and I want to make sure to share them with you and continue our open and honest relationship. Don't get me wrong, the good times far outweigh the bad, but I was stuck in a dark place for several weeks following my retirement and I don't want anyone to be blindsided by a similar situation.

Deciding to Leave the Rat Race

I never planned to retire at age forty-five. However, life often has its own plan, and as my story goes, my passion and talent were no longer welcomed at a job I loved. One morning I was given the chance to either claim retirement, or simply go get another job.

I thought about it for about thirty seconds until I decided I was done. It was time to turn the page and see where I wanted to go next.

This quick decision lead to about two days of excitement that I now refer to as a postretirement sugar high. Seemingly everyone I knew was reaching out to congratulate me on my new retirement status and I was grinning from ear to ear. I was finally cashing in after fifteen years of sacrifice, commitment, and execution. It felt so good, and from the outside looking in, it probably looked like nothing could go wrong.

As we all unfortunately know, sugar highs don't last, and they are often accompanied by a crash. I was no exception. I went from riding high on those two days of sheer joy to sinking into six weeks of downright depression.

My internal self-talk became increasingly negative as the days went by. See, my self-worth and ego were tied up in my job. My career is where I would get my daily endorphin rush of a job well done, and when that was taken away, I knew I had to find a replacement or my depression could have gotten really bad. Upon reflection, these dark days were probably inevitable since I ended up retiring very suddenly despite not having planned for it to happen until years later.

Two Choices

It was a rough six weeks as I beat myself up every day with negative self-talk. I was telling myself that I was lazy, no good, and lots of other nasty things no one should ever say about themselves. As I struggled with my mental state, it became clear I had two choices: I could either give up on this retirement nonsense and get another paycheck job, or I could embark on a new life journey that would be unknown and unscripted.

I ended up meeting with a few software company executives that I knew from previous jobs, with the knowledge that one option to dig myself out of this dark hole was to get another leadership job.

I never actually attended any formal interviews, but I was offered several exciting positions if I wanted them. Several CEOs and founders told me that they wanted me to be part of their team, be it on a full-time, part-time, or consulting basis. This felt great and reassured me that my passion, execution, and focus were still valuable and needed in the industry.

My other option was to build a new life, one that was 100% foreign to me but offered me unlimited options if I cared to commit. I had the opportunity to hop off the employee track and climb onto the entrepreneur track. This was a little scary, partly because my personal network is full of "employees." Don't get me wrong, plenty of my contacts are very successful people, but truth be told, they all work for companies. I had no frame of reference for the new path I had the option of taking, but I knew it was an option worth exploring.

With Olivia's help, I made the decision to commit to this second track. This meant telling all the senior executives with whom I was speaking that I would not be rejoining the employee ranks in 2018. I will take stock on January 1 of the following year and reconsider if my new plan doesn't work out, but until then I am 100% committed to this new goal.

What Got Me Out of the Dark Place

First, I have never been a person to suffer from depression or negative self-talk. However, when unplanned surprises happen, things can change and it can get ugly fast. Please make sure you check on friends and family whose lives have taken an unexpected turn, as things can get really weird when you are hit with a surprise you didn't plan for.

Two things got me out of my dark place. The first was informing the various executives I had been meeting with that I was truly out of the job market. This decision was surprisingly impactful, as I had been unwittingly feeding my gloomy mindset by looking at all the possible jobs that I would love and be great at. Every morning I would get up before 6:00 AM and spend hours outlining how I could help this or that company enter a new market or crush a competitor. I would then try and flip my mental focus to something else, and boom!—I was trapped between two worlds.

The second thing that helped me was refocusing my energy on a new target. Now that I no longer had a job, paycheck, or quota to focus on, I needed a specific goal to work toward.

This realization came to me during a conversation with Olivia about turning our fifteen-year journey into a roadmap for other full-time employees. This conversation sparked the One Rental at a Time book idea and growing YouTube channel, and has led me to participate in podcasts, speaking engagements at local real estate investing clubs, and so much more.

I've now made it my focus to tell the One Rental at a Time story to as many people who can benefit, as I believe every full-time employee can secure at least four rental properties with conservative financing.

One Rental at a Time

In order to help people achieve this goal, I have created a target of securing 10,000 YouTube subscribers by end of 2020 for my One Rental at a Time YouTube channel. This is the platform I update with short videos focused on some aspect of real estate at least five days a week.

To make this channel work I would like to request a few things from you.

First, please subscribe to my channel.

Second, please share the channel with your friends and family.

Lastly, please interact with me via a like when you watch a video, or better yet, leave a comment as I would love to hear from you. Please know I am a one-person show, so when you see a reply it came from me. Thank you!

The Book

First, I want to thank you for reading this book as it has been a labor of love and something I never thought about doing until it became clear that there are no books written by and for full-time employees who have invested in real estate to become financially free.

My vision for this book is pretty simple. I hope that every full-time employee who is looking for a way to retire picks it up and reads it a couple of times. I hope they are inspired by the first section and that they can see themselves in our story.

My hope is that the book inspires the action and confidence a full-time employee needs to obtain four solid affordable rentals that are conservatively financed and can be held for the long term.

Podcasts and Radio Shows

I'd love to be interviewed on any and all real estate related podcasts in order to share this story with the world. If you run a podcast and would like to have me on as a guest, please reach out (mzuber@OneRentalataTime.com). If you listen to a podcast and think I would have valuable input, please reach out to them and make a recommendation. I believe these are a great platform to tell stories, ask hard questions, and really dig into a topic, and I look forward to speaking on more of them each year.

Speaking Engagements

For me there is nothing more exciting than getting in a room full of like-minded people and telling our story, discussing real estate, or simply answering questions via panel discussions. If you run a real estate event with hundreds or even thousands of people in attendance, we should talk. Most of those attendees will be full-time employees and I want to help them and you by crafting a message that resonates with the audience. Please reach out to (mzuber@OneRentalataTime.com) if you have an event I should consider speaking at.

Website

I created www.onerentalatatime.com as a landing page. I haven't updated it in a while, as I have chosen to make my YouTube Channel the spot for nearly daily updates. I suspect I will need to update the site as I move forward but as a one-person show it is not lost on me that my website could use more of my cycles.

YouTube (Channel: One Rental at a Time)

I use YouTube as my main platform to share and communicate with my followers. I chose it because it provides an easy platform to create and post content across wide ranging topics.

I currently break my content into five different buckets:

1. PowerPoint presentations that communicate a point related to real estate investment. These videos range from 15 to 45 minutes in length and probably best listen to when you have a note pad or the ability to take notes.

2. Walkthrough videos of various projects in various states of repair. In one video I might take a three-minute walk through of a

disgusting slumlord property, and in the next video I might show you a completed Pride of Ownership rental. I share these conversions to help my subscribers understand the difference between a slumlord property and a quality, well-maintained rental.

3. Daily "Real Talk" videos. These are short five-minute clips that I record in one take as I walk my dog in the morning and riff on a topic. As the title implies, I give you my no-nonsense takes on various real estate related subjects, some of which might be uncomfortable as I touch a nerve or call something out. I intend these videos to be thought provoking and generally positive.

4. Subscriber questions, which I fully welcome and encourage everyone to participate in. Simply leave a comment or question on any of my videos, and I will very likely produce a video response within forty-eight hours. I really enjoy creating these and building a relationship with my subscribers.

5. Interviews. This component is just taking off but I hope to see it increase rapidly. There are so many ways to get involved in real estate, and I want to hear from people all over the world and with different experience levels. If you would like to be interviewed or know someone who would, please reach out to me at mzuber@OneRentalataTime.com .

The last point about my YouTube Channel is that I do everything myself. I do not have a team, so when you see a response it is coming from me and no one else. I have four simple requests:

1) Please subscribe to my channel!

2) If you enjoy a video or topic, please hit the like button.

3) Please share videos with your social network.

4) Please interact with me via leaving a comment or question.

Lastly, I have a Facebook page and an Instagram account called (you guessed it) One Rental at a Time. Today I post to them infrequently, but as I roll into 2019 and this book gets published I suspect I will create more material for these sites. However, YouTube will be my main platform for at least the next couple of years.

The Next Phase

Now that I didn't have a traditional job consuming eighty hours of my week, I was free to find something else to fill my days. I have never been the type to play golf every day (bad back), or grind at the gym for an ungodly amount of time (one hour is plenty). I had to do something to feel like I was contributing to society. Remember those dark days after leaving my job? I needed to find something that excited me and allowed me to feel like I was once again achieving great things day in and day out.

You probably already guessed that I chose to add to my real estate experience by adding flipping to my bag of tricks. If you remember from earlier in the book, I was never a "flipper," as it was too much work, too risky, and very cash intensive.

However, now that I have the time, the cash, and the connections, I thought it would be a good way to feel like a contributing member of society, and if I made a little money along the way, all the better.

The one thing I wanted to do in the flipping market was to create something new. I did not want to be like everyone else who bought a house, installed the fancy new items, and then looked to sell to an FHA buyer with 3% down.

Flipping to FHA buyers was not for me. It always felt like a maximum money grab, and at some point you knew a few of these properties would go back to the bank if the economy took a hard turn. I couldn't bring myself to feel good about putting a few extra dollars in my pocket and then hoping everything works out for the buyer.

Now, don't get me wrong. I understand that my responsibility to the buyer ends the day of the transaction closes, and I know why flippers focus on this market, but here is the deal: I don't need those extra dollars, and if I know that part of the market would cause me stress, why would I want to play in it? I won't, and I am okay with that.

If I didn't want to buy into the huge market of flipping to FHA buyers, what could I do?

I won't beat around the bush; I have decided to start flipping turnkey rental properties. Yes, you heard me right. I am buying run-down properties, spending $50,000+ remodeling them, leasing them at market, and then selling my *fully occupied and leased properties* to investors. I believe investors with full-time jobs and no time should buy and conservatively finance my flips, as they provide the best return-on-time and the lowest risk.

This little niche is great, and it feeds my soul in unexpected ways.

1) I get the joy of helping turn dilapidated properties into productive assets.

2) I get to help renters live in very nice properties that have been properly cared for and nicely put together.

3) I get to help very busy professionals secure their first or second property that is already repaired and fully leased. This gives them cash flow on day one and reduces their expenses for years to come.

4) When I choose to leverage an investment partner, I provide a very secure and timely return on their investment via my 6% and 20% program we previously discussed in this book.

When I first started to think about flipping properties, I wasn't all that excited. Sure, it was a way to make a few extra dollars, but that wasn't my motivation anymore. I had to find a way to feel good about what I was doing, and as it turned out, flipping to investors was the answer that creates a win-win outcome (see the four points above).

Turning Slumlord Properties into Pride of Ownership

The key to my flipping strategy relies on buying properties that are in what I refer to as "slumlord condition." These properties might be rented (but shouldn't be), or they might have been boarded up and vacant for years.

Properties in this condition need to be bought at the right price, or the model blows up. There are a lot of people looking for distressed properties in the current market, but in my market, I believe I am one of the few looking to create turnkey rentals. This allows me to be a little picky, as some properties will not make great owner-occupant flips, which reduces the competition.

The additional value of a property comes from what happens after acquisition, when we gut the property and start installing brand new fixtures. This includes brand new kitchens, bathrooms, flooring, and paint. We are also taking great care to put in items that will be landlord-friendly, like laminate floors and under-mount sinks, should there be a tenant turn. Anything we can do once during the remodeling process to reduce expenses later is good idea in my model.

These remodels often exceed $50,000 and generally take four to six weeks to complete, but the power of seeing the transformation is worth it. To date, the surest way to put on a smile on my face is to walk through a finished flip to see its unbelievable transformation. I feel great about every property we take from slumlord condition to Pride of Ownership quality.

Next is the easy part. Once we have a finished flip, it's time to lease the property at market rent. Given the top-notch condition of our rental units, attracting quality applicants has proven easy. Once the tenant moves in, we open escrow and start the close process with a buyer who has agreed to purchase the property once it has been repaired and leased.

Yes, you read that right. I do not have to put my properties in the MLS. I have investors (buyers) who reach out to me from across the country to ask to buy my flips. I am 100% focused on delivering fully leased and Pride of Ownership rentals to busy professionals so they can maximize their "return on time."

My buyers don't have time to mess around. They follow my model of conservative finance, long-term hold, and most are looking to acquire at least four rentals. I will discuss the "four rental" concept later, but in short, getting four investment loans is currently very easy and having four cash-flowing assets is a great way to expedite one's retirement.

If you would like to consider buying one of my Pride of Ownership rentals, please reach out to mzuber@OneRentalataTime.com so we can discuss what is right for you.

Go Slow?

As I rolled into this new chapter of my life, I was left with a nagging question. After three months of flipping, I had found six properties that would fit nicely into my business model of transforming slumlord quality properties into Pride of Ownership condition homes.

This proved that I could do it, but also gave me pause as I was left thinking, "Wow, what if I want to double or triple that number?" One part of my brain was telling me to go big, build a team, and become the largest real estate business in Fresno, while the other was telling me to be happy with what I had and reminding me that I didn't want to risk everything and move to Fresno; to think I could head the biggest real estate firm in a town without living there would be arrogant and foolish.

Frankly, I still struggle with this decision nearly a year later, and I have more or less decided that I need to focus on developing a legacy rather than on trying to earn more money. I'm at a point where I want to spend a couple of decades trying to help people, and I hope that in a hundred years some will still be reviewing my videos, books, blogs, and thoughts!

In the end, I look to complete around one project a month, and frankly I'll be happy if I only end up completing six a year. This will keep me busy, allow me to keep an eye on a changing market, and provide new and relevant content to my hopefully growing fan base.

At this point, One Property at a Time exists to help others and to create a legacy that outlives me by one hundred years.

Private Money Partners

As I was spinning this new business model of buying slumlord properties and turning them into Pride of Ownership rentals, I had to decide whether to raise private capital or to go at it alone. I had enough capital to do two projects at a time, but I was quickly learning that I would be able to find two properties a month that worked within the model.

I had the option to either buy the first two and then wait three to four months to buy the next two, or I could figure out a program that would better benefit my investment partners.

By leveraging private money I knew I could keep an assembly line of projects going at all times. Projects on average take between four to six months to complete, and if I bought two a month, I could have up to twelve projects going at one time.

This meant that I would have to raise private money if I wanted to keep feeding the machine. I spent time looking online and talking to other flippers about this, and the most popular approach seemed to be to borrow 100% of the purchase and 100% of the repairs, pay the lender a small monthly return, and then give them a small chunk of profit upon a successful sale.

I understand why flippers love this program, but I cannot for the life of me figure out why a private lender would like it. As I saw it, the lender took 100% of the risk while the flipper sat back and cashed a big check, a small slice of which they gave to the lender.

While I could clearly follow that program, that is not who I am. I would never ask my friends and family to invest in a program I myself would not invest in. For any private lenders who are saying yes to covering 100% of the purchase price and 100% of repair costs, you need to know that you are also taking 100% of the risk without 100% of the upside, which is just horrible math in my opinion.

I wanted to create a program that put my money at risk first, allowing my private lenders to be my true partners providing the absolute best security I could while keeping the assembly line of flips moving.

The 6% and 20% Program Is Born

The "6% and 20% Program" accomplishes this. It allows me to put my money at risk first, continuously recycle capital, and provide great security. Best of all, it allows the lender to be a true partner who benefits in our joint success. This is how it works in short, with hypothetical numbers as an example:

1) I buy a slumlord property for $100,000.

2) I close on that property by going through escrow, and I now own it free and clear, since I cut the check from my account.

3) I find a family friend who is "cash rich, asset poor," and we agree that they will loan me either $100,000 at 6% interest paid

monthly, or $500 in this example and receive 20% of the profit once the property is sold.

4) I then fund 100% of the repair costs out of my pocket—I could never ask an investor to fund both the purchase and the repair. Lets say it cost $40,000 to create a Pride of Ownership rental.

5) I lease the property at, say, $1,500 a month after the remodel is complete.

6) I sell the property at $200,000, with $10,000 in transaction costs.

7) This leaves $190,000 to be disbursed ($200,000 less $10,000 in transaction costs). My loan partner will get their $100,000 back first, then I get my $40,000 repair costs back. This leaves $40,000 in profit, of which my partner receives 20% ($8,000), and I get 80% ($32,000).

The last point about this program is that it is designed to be short-term, with the average hold time being under six months. This means that the annualized returns on these very secure investments have exceeded 20%, which has made my investment partners very happy! It should be noted that I am very happy as well, as it has allowed me to do what I love: turning slumlord properties into Pride of Ownership rentals and empowering busy professionals to buy quality, fully-leased and cash-flowing properties. To me, this is the ultimate Win-Win-Win.

Little Nevada

I want to take a minute to reflect on my first flip after leaving the rat race.

I call this first property "Little Nevada." I bought another flip on Nevada Avenue about four weeks later and that I named "Big Nevada."

Little Nevada was decrepit on so many levels. It was occupied by a group of squatters that had kicked in the door and were living there for weeks on end. I never heard the full story but based on the huge bill I paid just to clean out the property, they had been there for months. Did I mention the place had no electricity or running water? The squatters evidently did their business anywhere they wanted. It was beyond nasty.

But hey, I buy slumlord properties and these are the terrible conditions that I am willing to take on.

I found this property via a local wholesaler who had locked it up for about $50,000. He offered it to me for $65,000, which I agreed to, giving the wholesaler a quick $15,000 profit for his assignment fee.

I closed on this property in ten days, and that is when the fun began. My team went over to the property to establish signed lease agreements, as squatters do have rights, especially in California. This is when the squatters got aggressive and threatening, and I suspect that this is when they knew the party was over, or at least soon to be over.

The situation escalated quickly, and my team was forced to call the police for their protection. That's when all hell broke loose. The squatters fled the scene, leaving the property vacant as they took off.

The police informed us that as the new owners, we were now required to secure the building and board up broken windows in order to ensure no further break-ins, to which we agreed. After those tense few minutes, the property was vacant and ready for its makeover.

A couple of things to note: if the squatters did not freely give up possession, we would have had to either offer cash for keys or go through the eviction process, which in California could take up to ninety days. I frankly expected to spend a couple of thousand dollars paying them to leave the property, but thankfully they vacated when they saw the cops.

The other point is the squatters never came back. I actually paid armed guards to patrol the property four times a day and three times at night in the off chance they decided to return. Fortunately they never did, and the six-week remodel went off without a hitch.

We had to gut the interior because it was so mistreated, costing us an excess of $60,000. After six weeks of hard work the property was beautiful, and you can find plenty of video evidence on my YouTube channel.

Once the property was completely remodeled, we had no problem leasing it to a nice family at $1,200 a month. This fully leased property was then sold at $169,000 to an investor who wanted a fully remodeled turn-key rental.

My investor took home an additional $7,000 in profit, leaving me with a $28,000 profit and the sheer joy of knowing I had successfully turned a former disgusting slumlord property into a Pride of Ownership rental.

Little Nevada will always be special to me as the proof point that I can focus on what I know and create a program that benefits everyone involved. Best of all, it helps me focus on helping busy professionals who suffer from CRAP (cash rich, asset poor). These folks are simply too busy and don't have the time to change their future, and I know I can help them.

Working With Wholesalers

As the story above indicates, wholesalers are a common source of deals in this market. A wholesaler is someone who actively seeks out motivated sellers via direct mail, cold calling, and door knocking. The wholesaler's job is to lock up a property via a contract that includes an "Or Assignee."

The "Or Assignee" allows the wholesaler to quickly find a cash buyer to take their place in the contract for an assignment fee. This fee can range from a few hundred dollars to tens of thousands of dollars. Note I once paid a wholesaler $60,000 for their contract.

It seems that lots of people see the money wholesalers are making and think it is an easy job—you mail out 10,000 direct mail pieces, get 100 phone calls, get 20 appointments, and net two contracts. It may have been that easy three or four years ago, but now with all the "gurus" talking about virtual wholesaling and flashing stacks of cash on Instagram, it has become a crowded market. I still believe wholesaling is very profitable, but it is just not as easy as these people make it look.

When working with a wholesaler, this is what you want to do.

First, reach out to them and tell them what you are looking for. The more specific the better. Don't just call them and say, "I want a deal." That doesn't tell them anything other than that you are new, and thus you will only get junk. The wholesaler takes their good stuff to their "trusted" list.

Instead say something like, "I am looking for a three-bedroom, two-bath house in this or that zip code. It can't be on a busy street, and should be delivered vacant and require less than $30,000 in make-ready costs." The easier you make it for the wholesaler to evaluate what is best for the buyer, the more likely you are to get a call.

See, the wholesaler's job is to quickly match cash buyers with properties they know will close. The last thing you should do is agree to buy a property and then fail to close. Now don't get me wrong, if you discover something that was unknown by all parties, like a leaky roof or a kitchen fire, then by all means cancel. However, if the property is just as advertised and you decide not to close after agreeing, you will never get a second chance. The wholesaler spends a lot of time and money attracting motivated sellers, and the only time they see any return is when they get their assignment fee at closing.

The wholesale world is small; experienced wholesalers in every market know each other, as they have been competing for the same properties for years. If you burn one bridge, there is a good chance you've burned all of your wholesaler relationships across the board.

Always remember: real estate investing is a people business.

Buying Out of the MLS

As I shared earlier, I bought most of our properties out of the MLS for the first fifteen years of our business. I had no special access, just the discipline to look nearly every day for over ten years.

I still focus on the MLS as a place to find deals on slumlord properties to flip. Of the deals I locked up this year, about half have come out of the MLS. The key to finding or creating deals in the MLS is to be active and to know your numbers.

The hard part comes from the fact that 99% of the properties in the MLS are not deals for my model, and the ones that are can be hidden and easily overlooked. Listings rarely come out and say, "Seller motivated: make an offer, any offer!" (2009-2010 was an exception).

If you are just getting started, I would suggest picking a zip code and looking for thirty days straight, building an excel file with properties and statistics, and ranking them from best to worst deal. This thirty-day activity will make you a better investor for sure, and you will start to see over- and underpriced properties.

The last thing I want to say about buying out of the MLS is that I rarely offer asking price. In fact, I find it is often wise to offer 20% of more *below* asking price, as I am looking to uncover seller motivation. If the seller says "get lost," that is totally okay by me. However, if they counter, I know there is at least some motivation to get this property closed.

If you are new or just getting started, pick a zip code and start building your knowledge. As you gain experience, feel free to share your findings with friends and colleagues. This sort of collaborative experience will build your confidence and make it so much easier for you to write up your first offer.

You Never Know

Something you learn very quickly in this business is that you never know where a surprise deal will come from. With this in mind, it becomes hugely beneficial to make it known to everyone you know that you are in the real estate investing business. You will soon see that both information and deals will start to flow your direction. I have had access to multiple off market deals simply because an acquaintance knew I bought rentals.

Never hide the fact that you are a real estate investor; in this industry, you won't be rewarded for being in stealth mode!

The Facebook Duplex

I ran into an unexpected deal myself earlier this year, when Olivia and I sat down to eat dinner at a local Chinese restaurant. I took out my phone as we waited for our food and saw that a Fresno agent had posted a Facebook listing of a boarded-up duplex at a reasonable price.

I immediately replied with a note of interest and then sent a separate direct message the agent. I told the agent that I was a cash buyer who would close in ten days, and that all I wanted was for him to represent me in exchange for a $15,000 discount off the purchase price. He replied that he would call the sellers immediately and get back to me in an hour.

Thinking nothing of it because I make tons of offers below asking price and most go nowhere, we put away our phones and went about having a great dinner. As we waited for the check, I checked my phone again to see a message stating that the sellers have agreed and have already emailed me a purchase contract. I signed the contract electronically and we opened escrow the next day.

The best part of getting this property under contract was that I had a list of three buyers looking for Pride of Ownership duplexes. I called the first name on my list to let them know I had just signed a contract, telling them everything I knew about the property and giving them a range for monthly rent and expected purchase price post-remodel. They were interested. Note that at this point it had been less than eighteen hours since I had seen the original Facebook post, and I had not even seen the inside of the property yet.

To keep a long story short, the property had all of the usual issues, requiring just over $40,000 in make-ready costs after adding a last-minute privacy fence. This wasn't required, but as always, I try to exceed expectations. I know that I myself would want that privacy fence, so we added it despite the $2,000 deducted from my profit.

I used my 6% and 20% program to recoup the purchase cost, and my investment partner earned $7,000 in profit upon selling.

The Facebook duplex story really played to my strengths and interests as an investor. First, I bought a distressed asset that needed a cash buyer. I leveraged an investment partner who was looking for secure and short-term returns, and produced an easy-to-manage turnkey Pride of Ownership rental for a new buyer. None of this would have happened had I not looked at Facebook real quick before I ordered my dinner. Not a bad deal at all.

The First Year

When I stepped out of my nine-to-five life abruptly, I knew I would be okay financially and that I could go get another job if I wanted one. However, I wasn't exactly sure what I wanted to do all day, and as I explained earlier, that lack of direction was not good for me.

That all changed when I got serious about two things.

First, I focused on adding profitably flipping properties to my bag of tricks. I had long seen flippers in Fresno do great things, and I was unsure if I could do the same type of thing from 2 ½ hours away.

Second and most importantly, I got serious about crafting a legacy based on our "One Rental at a Time" story. I knew our story worked, and I knew it could help plenty of people if they took the time. However, a fifteen-year story that involves sacrifice and financial discipline is not exactly ideal for today's world of Instagram posts and Facebook updates that only talk about the good times.

Nonetheless, that is what makes it fun and critically important.

As I wrap up this section, I want you to know that I am 100% focused on trying to help as many people as I can take control of their lives. I hope to empower everyone to one day achieve financial independence, and know that it is possible with solid execution and time.

I appreciate in advance anything you do to help spread the story of One Rental at a Time. I'd love to start a #OneRentalAtATime hashtag!

Eleven Key Ideas

I want to close on some themes that have become important to me. It should be noted that these ideas have only begun to crystalize after thousands of conversations with investors, and from feedback on early drafts of this book.

These eleven concepts drive the majority of what I create and publish on a daily basis.

Let's begin.

1. C.R.A.P. = Cash Rich, Asset Poor

The first concept I want to discuss is a condition I see in too many people and families. Some people believe they can save their way to a comfortable retirement. They feel comfortable knowing they have $10,000, $50,000, or $100,000 in a savings account.

Unfortunately, I believe that trying to save your way to retirement goodness only guarantees disappointment. See, inflation is currently running higher than the interest rate you are earning in your savings account. This means that you lose money every day, week, and month, because inflation is causing the value your savings to be worth less as time goes by.

I find being cash rich and asset poor (CRAP) to be particularly frustrating, as these individuals are just one step away from taking firm control of their futures. If they can find a way to buy just a few assets that produce cash flow, are conservatively financed, and are able to hold for the long term, they will be a lot better off in the future.

Now, I don't want these people to buy into the maximum leverage story that is sold as a get-rich-quick scheme. Instead I recommend putting more money down and being very conservatively financed, which makes long-term hold an easy proposition. I find individuals and families that suffer from CRAP to be risk averse with very little time to commit to asset review and management. Thus, they need to hear that it's okay to be conservatively financed and holding for the long term. When individuals and families convert some of their cash into assets that are conservatively financed and easy to manage, they are changing their future for the better.

2. A.R.C.H. = Asset Rich, Cash Happy

When I think about what I want for my followers, I often come back to the acronym A.R.C.H., or asset rich, cash happy. This concept means two things.

First, it means that you are taking action by converting cash into long term assets that are conservatively financed. I believe that this is the key to a happy future and a safe and secure retirement.

Second, I believe that the only way out of the rat race is to do what rich people do day in and day out. It's my theory that the rich spend their time evaluating assets that produce cash flow and long-term wealth. For the average person, the best option is conservatively financed rental properties that produce cash flow from day one.

To be very clear, I never want any of my investors investing for appreciation. It is never okay to lose $100 a month because the property will be worth "X" more in "Y" time. I saw people lose everything in the great real estate collapse, and it was only because our properties produced cash flow that we could hold our portfolio and continue buying hand over fist during the crash.

Being asset rich and cash happy should be the goal for all my readers and followers (CRAP is bad, ARCH is the Goal).

3. No Alligators

I've been railing against alligators throughout this book, so I won't rehash what it means but instead focus on why.

During the real estate collapse, once-wealthy property owners started to see their portfolios collapse and their finances devoured by alligator properties.

The stress on people and their families was evident everywhere, as people were losing properties and robbing Peter to pay Paul in the hopes of holding on for another month. It was horrible to see friends lose everything. People who were worth $10 million or more were suddenly bankrupt as their alligator properties ate them alive.

The only reason we were able to escape the carnage and even profit was that every property we owned produced cash flow without help. We could in theory hold forever even if the property was worth less than some alligators. When your property cash flows and you have conservative long-term financing, its value from year to year doesn't really matter.

In the end, our net worth did fall big time during the real estate collapse but it just didn't matter. We believed our income statement was far more important than our balance sheet.

I can't close out this topic without reiterating this one more time: never buy or create an alligator property!

4. Conservative Financing

When I look at the real estate investment books on the market, the one topic where I seem to deviate most from the common practice is around *leverage.*

Most authors want to sell the sexiness and sizzle of building a portfolio fast. They show you spreadsheets with great numbers, and boom, you're paying for their $100 real estate class.

While the math in their spreadsheets generally make sense, I fundamentally don't believe in maximum leverage. Frankly, I think maximum or even high leveraging can be fatal and blow up your entire portfolio.

Given this, I like to talk about conservative financing. I want everyone following recommendations to use very conservative financing. If you are C.R.A.P. (cash rich, asset poor) and work a demanding full-time job, I want you to put at least an extra 10% down.

Why?

It's simple. Your investments have to run on autopilot if you don't have time to actively manage your portfolio, so it's wise set them up with very conservative financing. For example, some of my early investors are putting up to 50% down on their investments to make sure their assets perform every month.

This type of financing isn't sexy, but it helps convert cash into assets quickly. The investor is then set up for a long-term hold, and the other 50% of their cash flow asset is paid off by the tenant. Not a bad deal.

Please note that I am not recommending everyone put 50% down, but be conservative. For example, if the bank approves you for an 80% loan (you put down 20%) I want you to think about putting down 30% or 35% instead.

By doing this, you set yourself up to control an asset that easily performs year after year.

Before I get all kinds of hate mail, I know this kind of strategy means your returns are lower and your growth is slower. I am not trying to preach high leverage and fast growth. Instead, I want to teach low stress, easy cash flow, and long-term hold through any market.

5. Long Term Hold

The key to the investing philosophy I executed over the course of fifteen years hinges on putting yourself in a position to hold for the long term. Real wealth comes from owning assets for the long term; it takes time for tenants to pay off your asset and for inflation to make a difference.

As I shared earlier in the book, I do not suggest that full-time employees with small slivers of time try to take on "flipping properties." It is too risky, takes too much time, and is very easy to lose money to, regardless of what you see on TV.

Instead I suggest you focus on buying turnkey Pride of Ownership Rentals that are already leased at market, on which you use very conservative financing hold for the long term. If you can hold three to five income-producing assets for decades, you will take control of your financial future.

6. Inflation Is Your Friend

The last variable we need to appreciate in the "long term hold" framework is inflation. For most people, inflation is a dirty word that raises the cost of living and reduces your money's purchasing power.

However, as a real estate investor who is in this game for the long term, inflation is going to help you out on so many different levels.

1) The value of your asset is going to increase substantially over time. It might go down in any one year because of outside forces, but over twenty years your property will undoubtedly be worth a lot more.

2) Rental fees will go up over time. While any one year might be flat, your rental amount in twenty years will be a lot higher.

3) You will be leveraging conservative fixed-rate debt, which means you are locking in costs at today's level but paying off the loan with future dollars that are worth less.

In the end, inflation will single-handedly increase both your net worth and your monthly cash flow by significant percentages over two to three decades.

7. Get to Four

As I shared our One Rental at a Time story with increasing numbers of people, I learned that I need to modify my punchline.

In the beginning, I thought people wanted to hear about financial freedom and our growth to a large unit count. While people loved the story, it also became obvious that it wasn't necessarily inspiring people to take action, as they couldn't see a path from owning one rental to owning multiple units. We never saw a path either when we started, so it was easy to understand how our story could paralyze some people.

To that end, I have revised the goal of our story to taking this critical first step. In today's lending environment, that means we want new investors thinking about simply acquiring four rentals over a two to four year period. That's it. We want to help people get to four properties, and then we can see what is next.

If any investor can hold four properties in their portfolio, they have taken a huge step to controlling their future. Tenants will pay off their investment over time, inflation will increase their properties' value, and when they pay it off they will have plenty of cash flow and a high net worth to boot.

This will give them options. They can stand pat and use the cash flow. They can get a new non-taxable loan, sell a property, or simply exchange it into bigger properties.

In the end I want all readers of this book and those that follow me on YouTube to simply think about getting to four properties as they start their journey. Once you've achieved that milestone, we can talk about setting a new goal.

8. Middle Class Mindset

The more I talked to people from all over the country, the more it became clear that we have a mindset that is working against us every day. For some reason, this only hit me after I left my nine-to-five job.

In fact, the "middle class mindset" kills dreams every day.

This mindset can be summarized by mantra my mother would repeat every morning when she dropped me off at school:

"Now Michael, go get a good education, so you can get a good job, so you can make a lot of money, so you can buy lots of nice things."

To be clear, my mother was not doing anything malicious at all! She clearly loves me and sacrificed more than I can imagine to raise me. Love you Mom, if you ever read this! However, this mindset of "earning income so you can spend money on things" is what I refer to as "the middle class mindset," and I worked decades to rid myself of it.

Instead of making money to spend it, we should be thinking about earning money to save and invest in productive assets like the rich do.

The rich buy assets that rise in value over time and produce income streams that benefit them and their family for decades to come. The middle class buy depreciating assets, live above their means, and are broke at the end of the month.

The middle class mindset is especially dangerous today because of the Instagram, Snapchat and Facebook trend of flashing luxury products. People are not taking pictures of their studio apartment when they could afford a house, or taking photos of their Ford when they could buy a Mercedes.

From what I've seen, the investment phenomenon that seems to most celebrate sacrifice and reward frugality is the FIRE movement: *financial independence, retire early.* The research I have done on this movement is encouraging. It focuses on reducing expenses in a big way in order to achieve financial independence. My hope is the FIRE movement takes off and blossoms to something that is talked about and celebrated at dinner parties.

In the end I firmly believe it is the middle class mindset that is keeping most of us in the rat race. It is only when we step back and make some sacrifices that we can start to execute a plan for early retirement.

9. *Quality Differences of Real Estate Assets*

I had to include this topic in my closing section, as it was one of the areas that slowed us down when we began all those years ago.

When I started investing I was initially drawn to cheap properties. I assume it has something to do with my infatuation with penny stocks I had way back when. I got lost in the excel math of appreciation and value creation instead of in the reality of my bank account balance.

What I mean to say is that in the beginning, instead of asking myself how best could I use my cash, I let a spreadsheet drive my decision making. Like most of you, I was "cash constrained" in the beginning, and as soon as I bought one or two properties I knew I was going to be done for a while as I rebuilt my cash reserves.

Looking back now, this is where my mistake began. I thought that if I bought the cheapest property I would be in the best position to move forward to the next one. Wrong!

I should have bought nicer buildings, not taking into account that the bank was financing 80% to 90% of the investment property I was buying. I am embarrassed to say that I repeated this gaffe over and over again, and worse yet, it only became obvious when I looked back on our fifteen-year journey. Here is an example of a house I bought, and how it consumed too much cash and severely stunted our growth.

House I bought	What I could have Bought
Purchase Price $125,000	Purchase Price $160,000
Down Payment $25,000	Down Payment $32,000
Make-Ready Cost $20,000	Make-Ready Cost $0
Total Cash $45,000	Total Cash $32,000

Given that my biggest constraints were cash and time, I should have bought cleaner properties. I would have used less cash, and my time to cash flow would have been faster.

This simple yet powerful realization is why I chose to create fully leased turnkey Pride of Ownership Rentals that produce rent the day we open escrow. I have found that too many people have no time but have cash and a desire to move their financial future forward, and someone needs to help them.

I can't see myself ever running a big company, but if I can turn two dozen slumlord properties into Turnkey Pride of Ownership rentals a year, I will be doing my part to help busy professionals start off better than I did all those years ago. Feel free to let me know if you might be interested in purchasing one of these rentals.

10. Affordable Rentals

I want to remind you that if you follow my model, we do not buy Boardwalk or Park Place. We do not want to add these high-end properties to our portfolio; since they are risky and hard to cash flow.

Instead, focus on buying *below the median* in your market. Most markets are not creating new affordable housing stock, and thus supply is shrinking while demand is rising. This leads to higher rental rates and even better returns as time goes by.

Lastly, focus on property types that provide the greatest security and protection to your initial investments. This means buying affordable rental properties somewhere between 75% and 90% of the median for your market.

For example, if your market is like mine and has a median of about $260,000, I would like to see you buy only houses below $225,000. Doing this consistently will provide you with a low risk portfolio that is set up for cash flow for years to come.

11. Return on Time

The last topic I want to broach is a little different from anything I read about real estate investing when I started out.

Most of my readers' main constraint is time, not money. If time happens to be your main constraint, I want to offer up the idea that you at least consider "return on time" in your property acquisition process.

Let's look at an example from a friend who called and asked for advice. In this example, assume that the properties cost the same amount, the down payment was the same, and that my friend insists on self-management.

Friend: I need to review two properties with you. Property #1 is a nice fully remodeled building that is clean but will only provide $200 in cash flow a month. Property #2 is a value-add opportunity that needs work, but could provide $1,000 a month in cash flow.

Me: Interesting choices, but one question: didn't you just get another sales job with a territory that will cover several states? Would you say that Property #2 needs a lot more time, and potentially has a lot more make-ready costs?

Friend: Property #2 could take ten to fifteen hours a week to manage properly for that $1,000 a month. I'd also need to vacate the property and remodel the units. Not sure what that will cost but my estimate is $25,000 to $40,000.

Me: Ok, so I know you have the cash, but I am here to tell you that you don't have the time to take on such a project. I promise you one of two things will happen if you purchase Property #2: either your job will suffer or your rental will suffer. You can't take on a project that requires active involvement when you don't have the cycles to spare.

Friend: This is true. I got lost in the huge cash flow instead of thinking about how I spend my scarce time.

Me: Great! I suggest you either buy Property #1 or you keep looking. Property #2 is a nonstarter and should not be considered any longer.

In Closing Thank you so much for reading. It means the world to me that you took the time to secure and complete the book. My hope is that you now believe that working full-time and investing in real estate can be a great side hustle that leads to a better retirement, and potentially, financial freedom.

In addition, I hope you see the importance of execution, conservative financing, and holding for the long term as keys to low risk and low stress investing.

Good Investing, and remember to subscribe to my YouTube channel for updates and thoughts about real estate.

Made in the USA
Monee, IL
31 August 2021

76973304R00095